*   *   *

Life Under Open Skies
Adventures in Bushcraft

by
Tony Nester

Life Under Open Skies: Adventures in Bushcraft

Copyright January 2015
ISBN: 978-0-9713811-5-5
Diamond Creek Press, Flagstaff, Arizona
2532 N. Fourth St. #313
Flagstaff, AZ 86004
Diamondcreekpress.com

Cover Art by Mad-Moth

Editing services provided by Emily Nemchick

Warning
The learning and practice of survival skills in both emergency and non-emergency situations can be dangerous. This book is not a substitute for sound judgment and common sense. The observations and comments regarding bushcraft and survival are presented here solely as general information and for entertainment purposes and not for application in the outdoors. The reader should undertake training with a qualified instructor before attempting any survival techniques. The author disclaims any liability from any injury that may result from the use, proper or improper, of the information contained in this book.

* * *

Life Under Open Skies
Adventures in Bushcraft

For my father—

thank you for teaching me the joy to be had

in working with my hands out on the land.

I wish I could show you what I've learned.

And to all my dogs that have been with me on

countless treks and taught me what it means

to truly embrace life.

Table of Contents

Prologue

On the dashboard of my truck are several plant stalks of weathered yucca. I can roll a piece between my hands and feel the woodsmoke of a campfire rush over me. A campfire started in the old way using a yucca stalk for the fireboard and the spindle to create the uniquely human miracle known as fire by friction. When I am out hiking and a yucca appears on the trail, I feel an instant connection and sense of gratitude for a plant that has given me warmth on many cold nights, fed me, and provided so much. Yucca is a trusted desert friend.

Each of us belongs to a particular place and land—a place that your soul swims in. I grew up in the Great Lakes region and fell in love with the outdoors at an early age, but it wasn't until I took a train out west to work in the Great Basin during my early twenties that I was grasped deeply by the pulse of the desert. That first trip to those sagebrush-shrouded mesas turned me into a permanent desert wanderer and opened my eyes to a much larger world.

I believe that we have several birthplaces in life—the physical setting where we are born into this world and the spiritual birthplace that is our true home, *the* place we are meant to reside and where we will flourish. For me, coming home was finding the desert.

I didn't grow up as a gully-jumping country boy with a bow and arrows in my hands, nor did I have a fictitious Indian mentor who took me under his wing. My family lived in the suburbs north of Detroit where my father worked in the tool-and-die trade making a living with his hands in the days before robotics. There were woods around our neighborhood back in the 70s, and I spent every minute in them building forts and learning about the birds, animals, and plants.

When I was eleven, my parents enrolled me in a local Boy Scout troop and my journey into the world of bushcraft commenced. We had two crusty woodsmen who ran the troop and they had us camping out in every season practicing traditional and modern camping skills. From axmanship to fishing, Dutch-oven cooking to snow camping and foraging for wild plants—I learned how to become a junior woodsman.

Those formative years in the Scouts provided a foundation in the baseline skills for being confident in the outdoors. It also expanded my vision of what the natural world offered to those who knew where and how to look. As with most fields, no matter how "advanced" you become at your craft, it will always be the basics that you fall back on, and I still rely on those early Scouting skills today. Bushcraft opened up a world of possibilities that I was unaware of with modern camping, which is so gear-dependent and revolves around separation from one's surroundings rather than immersion.

After high school, I tried attending college but being indoors just wasn't for me (it didn't help that I was reading Thoreau and Whitman either). The real world unfolded outside of the academic walls and every fiber in me yearned for the backcountry. I dropped out of college and took to the woods of northern Michigan and the deserts of the West. For years, I traveled the country learning from whomever I could, earning money by working for wilderness youth rehab programs and summer camps. I'd work for a few months and then take off to another new wilderness region I'd learned about. I spent much of those four years living in tipis, numerous caves, cabins, wickiups, and the back of my vehicle. It was an apprenticeship in bushcraft and in life on the open road.

After many moons of dwelling under open skies and eventually getting burnt out on working adjudicated youth programs, I decided to go back to school to get a degree in anthropology. Many of the outdoor education jobs at the time required a Bachelor's degree and my wilderness experience wasn't enough to get anything beyond entry-level teaching positions. Anthropology was intriguing and I knew it was the only subject that would hold my interest long enough to stay indoors. As an older student, I was ready for college and was extremely focused on my studies. Having spent so many years enmeshed in primitive living, I wanted to learn the academic side of our human heritage. I spent my summer months off in Michigan's Upper Peninsula whose wilderness rivals that of the western US.

As fate would have it, in my senior year of college, a friend and I were asked to head up a new program in primitive technology for the Ojibwa and Potawatomi tribes near Sidnaw, in the Upper Peninsula. I was humbled to undertake such a teaching venture. For seven summers, during Northern Michigan University's Native American Science Program, we taught daily workshops to indigenous youth in flintknapping, sheltermaking, fire by friction, weaving, plant uses, outdoor survival, and animal tracking.

For the first three years, we were definitely viewed as outsiders and kept at a distance by the older members of the tribe who were used to too many experiences with *wannabes*. When the fourth season began, something clicked and we were suddenly invited to drumming circles and campfire ceremonies along with being introduced to more of the traditions of the Anishinaabe people.

When my wife and I eventually moved to Arizona, we found, much to our excitement, that many of the traditional skills that had been lost to native cultures further east, where contact with Europeans occurred earlier, were still intact amongst the Southwest tribes. Friends up at Hopi have recounted stories of growing up hunting rabbits with throwing sticks, making juniper bows for deer hunting, using deadfall traps, and crafting traditional basketry.

Learning how to live in the wilds with your hands and a few tools can be likened to learning a new language. As with any language, after time the psyche becomes saturated with the nuances of that culture and you feel a subtle paradigm shift occur as thought patterns change and you begin to see the world through a different lens. One does not have to venture around the globe to enter another culture. It is right on your doorstep waiting to be explored within the trees, birds, animals, plants, and other inhabitants of that exotic land known as Nature. You enter a wild place that has its own laws, and each environment, whether desert, mountains, jungle, forest, or Arctic, has its own unique dialect and even subcultures. I'm realizing as I get older that ten lifetimes would scarcely be enough to comprehend the *linguistic* flavor of even one of these environments. I long to stay put now so as not to miss out on something happening locally out my back door.

Later, when I became better grounded in the basic skills and knew the land where I lived, I began to take to the wilds at every opportunity, bringing a minimum of gear while seeking a new river or canyon to explore. Over the years, I have gone out on solo treks spanning a month while taking only a knife, cooking pot, and a small sack of rice. The rest came from nature's kitchen, and many times I went hungry, but it was all for the sake of learning and expanding my skills.

During such outings, one quickly realizes how few things are needed to truly live but what an absolute treasure those things are. As one of my students remarked after participating in our nine-week traditional skills program, "*I've accomplished so much with so little; now I can do almost anything with just my hands and a knife!*"

To learn a new language it helps to have a teacher fluent in the field. It is important to research the background of the person teaching and learn what their particular angle is. There are schools run by ex-military instructors, new-age teachers, native philosophy instructors, primitive technologists, and outdoor educators. Some of these are schools that focus on technical proficiency with the physical skills while some dwell on spirituality and meditation, and then there are the "push yourself to the limits" schools that focus on endurance and hardship to promote character development.

For myself, I have always been drawn towards the hands-on skills and the thrill of living off the land for extended periods of time. It's been my experience that if you learn the skills first, then the suffering factor is reduced. Having been a student and an instructor on endurance-type survival courses, I can tell you that the learning curve plummets when you are cold, hungry, dehydrated, and cursing the staff. You shouldn't have to pay someone to suffer—you can do that on your own for free!

Many of the musings and stories that follow come from personal treks or extended fieldcourses during the past twenty-five years of being involved in the study of bushcraft. I hope you enjoy the ride. It has been a grand adventure with many more trails ahead.

Tony Nester
Flagstaff, Arizona
January 2015

* * *

Bare Bones Survival

One sunny April afternoon, I received a call from a Hollywood agent inquiring about survival training. The agent informed me that she had an actor named Emile Hirsch who was to play the lead role in the film adaptation of the book *Into The Wild* directed by Sean Penn. Emile wanted to prepare for his portrayal of Chris McCandless, the young explorer who ventured into the Alaskan bush to live off the land and later died of starvation. After speaking with Emile about his goals, we arranged a training date in May.

A month later, Emile flew into Flagstaff to participate in a private, knife-only survival course. When I picked him up at the airport terminal, I barely recognized him from his movies. He was gaunt from months of aerobic training and a restrictive diet in order to lean him out for the movie's final scenes of starvation.

We drove downtown for dinner where we discussed the specifics of the training course. Emile came across as self-confident and inquisitive with a lack of ego. He was clearly passionate about not only acting but his involvement in this particular film. Emile indicated that he wanted to focus on hunting with a .22 rifle (McCandless had one), finding edible plants, firemaking skills, primitive fishing, and spending a night out with only the clothes on his back. He also had many questions about my long solo treks and the psychology of being alone in the wilderness.

We headed into the forest the next morning and ran through all the basic skills. When we weren't working with our hands, we were walking the land in search of rabbits. As the sun faded, we returned to camp and mulled over the fate of McCandless and what had drawn people to his story for so many years. I commented how it's easy to get in over your head when you are first venturing into the wilds on your own, especially if you have your head filled only with book know-how rather than actual field experience.

Emile was a real gentleman and an astute learner with a great sense of humor. He picked up the skills quickly and slept in a handmade shelter without the benefit of a sleeping bag or blanket. It was in the 20s that night and he must have been cold given his low-calorie diet, but he never complained.

If you pursue the field of bushcraft long enough, there comes a point when the urge to take to the wilds and provide for all your needs for a long duration rises to the forefront of your thinking. I am not talking about an overnight survival outing or eking out an existence munching on grasshoppers and dandelions. Rather a period in one's development as a bushman where you have thoroughly grasped the basics and want to apply them with the most exacting master teacher of all: Mother Nature. She's the one who provides immediate (and sometimes unpleasant) feedback on where you stand, and she is impartial to the survival school certificates, cool gear, and all of the Youtube videos you've digested. Learn the basic skills, ease yourself into the wilderness in baby steps, and work towards being a well-rounded woodsman. Look at bushcraft as a lifetime pursuit and remember that you, as a modern human, are trying to learn what took our ancestors decades to master and the collective effort of a tribe.

Amongst my university students, the story of Chris McCandless still has a strong pull. The romantic notion of casting off the restraints of urban life and heading into an untrammeled wilderness to re-invent yourself is one that permeates the American psyche, especially amongst the younger generation.

Emile stayed on for another day of training and then headed off to Alaska to begin primary filming. When the movie *Into the Wild* came out, I thought he did an amazing job of transforming himself for the grueling role. I was deeply moved and saddened by the film and it's a story that I wish had a different ending. I recall how Emile said that when he initially began interviewing Alaskans about this tale, most would recount that McCandless was but one in a continual strand of wilderness seekers who would disappear into the bush never to be heard from again. This desire to cut ties and wander alone clearly has deep roots in the psyche, perhaps stemming from our hunter-gatherer past when we ventured off on our own during late adolescence to test our mettle apart from the tribe. Such rites of passage for young men and women are sorely lacking today.

I'll admit that I was fascinated with doing a long solo experience after high school when I ventured into the wilds with just the clothes on my back. After graduation my head was filled with romantic notions about wrestling a livelihood from the natural world. I bid my folks farewell and headed to the wilds of northern Michigan. My plan was to live off the land for three weeks with a minimum of gear such as clothing, handmade moccasins, knife, cooking pot, firestarter and just my hands along with a pint of know-how (or a few ounces of it anyway).

There was a small lake east of the town of Grayling that I had camped at many times with a friend's family and I knew this would provide both the natural resources and isolation I was craving. The only problem was that the fantasy world in my head didn't exactly mesh with the reality provided by the cold, mosquito-infested forest that I walked into with my starry eyes. But survival is only adventure in retrospect and I was due for a hard slap in the face.

After parking my car and walking a few miles to the lake, I built a lean-to from oak branches and fallen leaves. Once the primitive abode and adjoining fire pit were completed, I sauntered down to the lake to gather cattails and fish. I'm pretty certain that the lake had recently thawed from its icy spring grip as my legs were numb within minutes of wading in to gather cattail shoots. The only fish to be seen always stayed out of reach, thus thwarting my notions of primitive angling. A later attempt to procure them with a nifty fish spear did little to quell my hunger pangs. That night, as I sat in my shelter feeding the fire and starving my body, I fashioned a few throwing sticks from sugar maple branches. With a new plan, I would greet the sunrise with a morning hunt for rabbits. Surely they would be easier fare than the elusive panfish that mocked me from a distance.

By noon the next day, my lengthy hunt had only yielded sore feet and a rapidly shrinking stomach. I filled my belly with water from a nearby spring and staggered back to my lean-to. With a plummeting energy level and a foul mood, I snacked on the remaining roasted cattail roots while a cloud of mosquitos used me as their culinary pin-cushion. Experiencing a season of North Woods flying bloodsuckers is only slightly better than sleeping on a pile of jagged rocks in the rain. After a day of this airborne assault, my ravaged skin resembled cork and I reprimanded myself for failing to bring repellent to protect my mottled skin.

The only respite from the legions of winged vampires would be to increase the size of my smoky fire. After piling on damp wood and green pine-needle sprigs, the mosquito problem was finally abated—for about three minutes, at which point I required an intake of oxygen. This required me to alternate between bathing in the thick smoke and taking occasional fresh-air breaks a few feet away. The mosquitos seemed to know precisely where the demarcation line between the two realms existed so I had to determine if succumbing to smoke inhalation was worse than becoming anemic.

By evening, I pulled my sooty, swollen face from the fire and strode down to the lake to gather more cattails and see if any fish might show me mercy by swimming closer and floating on their sides. At least the cattails couldn't run or hide from me so I ended up dining on more roots that night. By midnight, I was awoken by a terrible grumbling noise, the kind that a gastroenterologist might refer to in a medical class. My field guide to edible plants didn't say anything about how many cattails to eat before the high-fiber scale tipped out of your favor. Most of that night was spent sprinting from my shelter towards the nearest tree. In between the countless hasty extractions from my lean-to, I wondered how fledgling mountain men fared during their first season afield. Of course if they were in my situation, they probably would have walked back to the car.

The next morning while lying in my coffin-like shelter, the ridgepole of which was coated black from the constant haze of resinous smoke, I pondered my mental checklist from earlier in the week, prior to my departure. It read much differently than I expected when I was sitting on the couch back home.

That earlier list looked like this:

- Procure assorted panfish for breakfast and dinner.
- Kill 2-3 rabbits during mid-day jaunts.
- Make a finely crafted bow and arrows around the evening campfire.
- Weave a willow basket and then gather a few quarts of berries (even though, in retrospect, berry season wasn't until August).
- Jerk or smoke surplus meat and fish.
- During leisure time, weave a large fishnet from handwoven rope.
- Rest, dream, plan future trips.

As one old woodsman told me, reflecting on life in the bush, "There's the way it oughta be and there's the way it is." Accordingly, here's what my newly modified list looked like:

- Attempt to catch or spear fish then gather cattails instead.
- Collect more damp firewood to keep bugs at bay.
- Attempt to hunt rabbits then gather cattails instead.
- Collect more damp firewood to keep bugs at bay.
- Stand in the woodsmoke while contemplating whether to hunt rabbits or spear fish then eat remaining cattails.

- Sleep, dream of slices of pizza that know my name, then sprint from my shelter once more to answer nature's call.
- Pile more damp wood on the campfire along with torching the remaining cattails.
- Pray for sunrise to come quicker than usual so I can walk back to my car and drive home.

To say the trip was dismal was an understatement. I left on the fourth day and drove home in silence, barely remembering the sights or towns along the way.

Upon arriving back in the suburbs, my parents greeted me with hugs. My father didn't say a word about how I had only been gone a few days and not three weeks but did remind me that the grass needed cutting. I came back not with a feeling of elation or a sense of accomplishment but with my soul crushed, my stomach the size of a walnut, and my body in need of a transfusion. I had done as Thoreau suggested and "driven life into a corner" but it seemed like that's where I was stuck and with plenty of cobwebs obscuring the way out.

The wilderness had been the one place in my life that I longed to be in and now that world was shut off through my own self-imposed defeat. The rest of the week I stayed inside as much as possible or did car repairs with my dad. I barely took notice of the house sparrows and cardinals outside my bedroom window and for once, I didn't know what direction the wind was blowing from on an hourly basis—one sign I had told myself was a sure indicator that you were a decent bushman. Now none of that mattered. As the week progressed, I grew to despise the outdoors and the old skills of woodsmanship. What was the point if only suffering was involved? Where were the glorious sunrises, the majestic hunts, the beauty of trees swaying in the summer wind? All of it was gone and now there was just life in the city left to contemplate.

A few weeks after my return I got a job at a local sporting goods store. It would be far easier to talk about the outdoors and the accompanying gear from the comfort of having a roof over my head—and there sure as hell weren't any bugs whining in my ear. This was the answer! I would work in the outdoor retail field and fill my hunger for the wilds vicariously without any discomfort.

For the next two months I plodded along, working my shift and waiting for some sliver of joy to emerge in between stocking fishing poles, slingshots, and boxes of ammo. One morning in late August, my mom gave me a section of the newspaper that had an article about the Porcupine Mountains in the western Upper Peninsula. I had heard of the rugged wilderness area before. That dormant longing for wild places began pushing its way up inside me like the first buds of spring. I put aside the article and forced myself back to the work routine but the notion of heading to the Porcupine Mountains kept prodding me, lingering like a spiritual signpost. While glancing at the sleeping bag rack at work one day, I thought, *Why not take some modern gear and just go backpacking?* It wasn't anything novel but for years I had told myself that, in order to have a pure wilderness experience, one had to forego the modern gear and rely strictly on traditional methods.

A week later, I quit my job, packed my car (a *backwoods* '79 Cutlass Supreme which shed chunks of rust with each bump in the road), and took off for a weeklong solo backpacking trip along Lake Superior by the Porcupine Mountains. Loaded with 60 pounds of ultra-modern gear, a gas stove, dehydrated food, and a fancy mummy bag, I hardly even saw the scenery because I was so hunched over from the weight. However, great weather, few mosquitos, solitude, lack of resinous woodsmoke, and lots of berry picking were to be had during those seven glorious days. With aching shoulders and a sore back, I realized that I had done a complete 180-degree pivot in my wilderness experience, going from the ill-equipped primitive outing earlier to a modern trek cocooned in pricey gear. I knew there had to be a middle ground but didn't know where to begin.

On my last leg of the trail on that final day of the hike, I was fiercely determined to learn how to live simply in the wilds and knew that I had to ease myself into the challenging study of bushcraft. There weren't going to be any shortcuts to mastery. Our ancestors had spent a lifetime learning to live off the land and with the help of countless mentors in their tribe, while I had attempted to go back twenty-thousand years in my disastrous weekend foray in June. Carrying disc-rupturing amounts of modern gear didn't seem like the answer either as it made me feel like a space explorer detached from the very surroundings I sought to connect with.

While walking the trail back to my car on the last day, I decided that I was going to devote the rest of my life to learning bushcraft. I would find the right way to live closer to the land without over dependence on gear and without the mindless suffering associated with mere survival. The next twelve years were spent in pursuit of the old ways while learning how to ease myself into the wilds incrementally and reducing my reliance on modern camping gear.

Once you have completed an extensive wilderness trek, where the ties to civilization have been severed and where the head and hands are your main tools, you will *know* that you can endure any hardship or privation in life and come out on top. And when, after trip's end, you glance at the tanned furrows in your face and hands, you will feel like a part of a much larger world. Today, I prefer blending the best of both modern and traditional skills and each trip offers the opportunity for continual refinement, though I still shy away from dinners comprised of cattails.

* * *

Guardian

It had been a long, hot day of exploration and I was exhausted. I should have been paying more attention to my surroundings. Six hours earlier, it started off as a serene September morning as a friend and I decided to bushwack to some prehistoric cave sites in central Arizona. This was a riparian zone I had been to before that housed an extensive array of 70+ caves in the limestone layer above a slow, meandering river.

According to archeologists I've spoken with, the site probably accommodated thousands of people in prehistoric times. These were the ancestors of the Hopi, often referred to as the Anasazi. The caves were sprinkled along three levels of rock formations. Most were honeycombed inside with two to three more caves.

Looking over the lush band of cottonwoods surrounding the site, it's not hard to imagine generations of children raised on the mesas, their days filled with foraging, trapping, and hunting along with tending small gardens of corn.

Rich and I parked a few miles away and did the arduous hike to the site. Crossing through patches of juniper, cholla, and crucifixion thorn made for slow going. Thankfully, this was also the main reason that busloads of tourists don't venture into this torturous and seldom seen region.

We arrived at the caves by early afternoon and immediately went to the river to soak our shirts and cool off. The temperature was in the mid-90s and it was the perfect time for a siesta under the shade of the mighty cottonwoods and sycamores. The area was comprised of ashen jagged hills that looked like the backbone of a dinosaur. The walls of the canyon, by the river bottom, seemed to muscle apart in the narrow stretch before us.

After downing some lunch, we headed up to the caves, a hundred yards away. Given the sinewy confines of the entrances, we found it better to split up and explore on our own. Regrettably, many locals have already pilfered the ruins over the years and little remains of the once voluminous amounts of prehistoric pottery that I'd seen years ago.

My main interest on this trip was not only to explore but to record the temperature gradient found within the caves to better understand shelter dynamics in the intense heat of the desert. Lava tubes and caves can often have a thirty degree temperature difference compared with the outside air. Such formations can be a lifesaver for a desert survivor stranded in an unforgiving landscape.

Several hours later, after poking around the alcoves, I was ready to leave and headed back down to the river to purify some water. Rich was still on the upper level and while waiting for him, I spied a row of four caves to the north that I'd missed.

I tanked up on water, donned my pack, and ambled up a faint animal trail that led to a small ledge by the caves. The entrance of each one was perhaps three feet in diameter, so I set my pack down and grabbed my flashlight. The first three caves were actually much larger than they appeared. Once inside I could see that they had roughly eight-foot ceilings and went back about fifteen feet with several more honeycombed chambers being evident. Given that the ground was littered with rodent droppings, I avoided investigating any further and pulled out to explore the last cave.

Due to the excitement of reconnoitering, I wasn't paying much attention to the tracks on the chalky soil at this point. I knelt down and crawled through the narrow entrance of the final cave, half-emerging into a small chamber. The feeling of cool sand beneath my hands soon faded as I heard the loud rattle of a snake off to my right. Slowly turning with my headlamp, I saw an immense diamondback rattlesnake coiled on a ledge beside the entrance; his sharply angled head was about eighteen inches from me. My neck felt like it had a bull's-eye painted on it, and I went from dealing with the heat to becoming numb with frostbite.

At that point I realized my life was going to be reduced to mere minutes if I got nailed on my carotid. My future was in the scaly figure of what I prayed was a seasoned old-timer who was more interested in packrats than a woefully unaware traveler. His agitated rattling continued and his head was poised high, making me think I should have noticed the "S" shaped tracks that could be clearly seen in the sand to my right.

With a heavy bead of sweat rolling off my temples and my heart punching through my chest, I spent the next few minutes performing a Tai-Chi extraction move which felt like it took most of the afternoon to perform. His rattling only let up once my shaken form was back in the sunlight outside. My body felt like I had just climbed a mighty mountain peak and I collapsed by my pack, gulping in the fresh air.

Rich, who was down below the ledge, asked why I was so pale and suggested that maybe I hadn't consumed enough water. I sputtered out the words, "Me, not thirsty." (Did I really say that?) After the adrenaline dump wore off and the coil of knots in my stomach unfurled, I grabbed my pack and stumbled down the trail to the river, where I dunked my head. The cool water cleared my throbbing skull enough to recall the advice, momentarily forgotten, that I give to my own students: "Don't put your hands and feet where you can't see." To that I would also add *your head.*

* * *
Flash Flood!

It was late August and ten of us were out on the first day of a seven-day bushcraft course near Winslow, Arizona. We had the good fortune of holding the course on a private ranch encompassing thousands of acres of rugged high-desert landscape complete with a perennial creek, rock art, and miles of narrow canyons.

Our small group headed out across the dunes on a hot afternoon as storm clouds were brewing to the south. Fortunately for us, the wind was from the north, keeping the storm in the opposite direction. It was an idyllic setting and we meandered up a small side canyon to our camp location, along the way stopping to gather cottonwood for carving friction-fire implements and bowls.

We arrived at a little bench of sandstone which was about seven feet above the canyon floor. It was a sandy shelf or *bosque* with some hackberry trees and Goodding's willows. Below it was a tiny trickle of water from the last rain storm. After a short discussion on shelters and poncho-rigging, people broke off to construct their abodes and make their primitive beds. Myself and the other instructors set about gathering firewood and other teaching materials while taking time to enjoy the myriad sets of tracks dotting the sandy canyon.

There was a gentle breeze blowing down canyon that made the temperature seem Mediterranean. It was a peaceful, serene setting and a great start to the week. The group was fantastic and very social which would make for a lot of good storytelling around the campfire.

As we started the fire for cooking dinner, the wind suddenly shifted 180 degrees and drew the distant storm cell down upon us. It was a massive cumulonimbus cloud and within minutes, the rain dropped in sheets and the sun shrank from our sights. Within ten minutes, the tiny rivulet of water in the canyon below us was transformed into a raging current carrying van-sized boulders and massive logs in its grip. So much for serenity and peace. We had to retreat to higher ground, which was one reason we had selected this camp, with its easy access to an escape route—a canyoneering habit you adopt early in the Southwest.

After accounting for everyone, we hastily gathered our belongings and gathered to discuss options. There was little point in staying where we were on the exposed bedrock, as the high ground offered little protection from the lightning storm enveloping us. I informed them that we would head south to the main canyon where there were large juniper trees for sheltering under. I told everyone to follow lightning protocol and spread out at least thirty feet from the person in front of them. This would help prevent the entire group from perishing from a lighting strike should one person get hit.

It was now nightfall and the landscape was dominated solely by two forces: the lightning which illuminated the glistening rocks beneath our boots and the roar of the canyon which had become a living artery of mud, logs, and giant rocks churning through the passage below. On calm days, it's easy to forget that this raw desert landscape so many of us love was shaped by violent forces. No reminder was needed in the moments that followed.

Amazingly, everyone was in good spirits and this night of adversity, which had only just begun, was to be the ultimate group building experience like no other I have experienced before or since. By the end of the day, this group of people who had been strangers only hours before were to become fast friends and gel into a tribe for the rest of the trip.

It was well over an hour before we made it to the confluence of the two canyons from which we had come. The main canyon had also flooded and, now combined with the side canyon where our camp had been, was swollen, making it impossible to safely cross. Despite my best efforts at planning and familiarity with the countryside, our escape route was cut off! The danger with flash floods isn't just the force of the water but all of the sediment, debris, and logs that have accumulated since the last scouring which, in some areas, can be decades apart. We were staying put—there was little choice.

We found the nurturing junipers with their welcome arms and sought shelter beneath them. Everyone changed into dry clothes and then we proceeded to get a fire going using a spark rod and cottonballs soaked in Vaseline to ignite the damp bark. The wood was saturated but we fell back on a technique I had learned years ago in the North Country which involved splitting open large sections of dead limbs. We then shaved the dry interior and ignited this for kindling. Juniper saved us that night and I had new respect for why the Navajo called it *Bittahatsi*: "the one that provides for us."

Clothing, boots, packs, hair, ears, nose, nails—all were laced with an amalgam of sand and water. The rain and lightning came and went throughout the long night. Most people doubled up and tried to sleep atop beds of duff under the junipers while survival-spooning together. I didn't sleep a wink, too much trip leader stuff floating through my brain—safety, hypothermia concerns, liability, new group dynamics, and the fact that it was only the first day and we had six more to go!

My mind raced back to the Antelope Canyon flash flood on the Utah/Arizona border that happened years earlier and the unfortunate hiking party that failed to pay heed to the warning signs. The slot canyon that the group of 12 hikers was exploring was bone dry with blue skies above. However, 15 miles away, a cloudburst sent a massive wall of water down canyon. A short time later the current engulfed all of the hikers. Only the guide made it out alive. He emerged wearing a single boot as his clothing was shredded away. In his attempt to rescue the others, he stayed behind in the swift-rising water which was filled with debris and heavy silt. The sandpaper action of the grit on his legs stripped away the outer layer of his skin and when he arrived at the Emergency Room in the town of Page afterwards, he was treated like a burn victim, so severe was the trauma. I reminded myself that we weren't in a narrow slot canyon and had chosen the area for its resources as well as its many escape routes but lying in the mud still wasn't appealing.

With thunder claps bellowing in the distance, I forced my mind back to the present. My thought was to let the group get some rest until sun-up but there was another storm looming in the distance and a repeat performance wasn't high on my list. Hopefully we'd be able to cross the swollen river before then. On the ebbing of the flash flood around 3 am, I gathered everyone up, crossed the ankle-deep water, and headed back out into the night to a dryer camp nearby.

Due to the entire desert landscape resembling brown pudding, we decided to head to a higher elevation in the forest and completed the duration of the course there under relatively drier conditions. Day one, which had begun in such an idyllic setting and drastically changed within minutes to raw elemental power, was nearly over. We found out later that the storm had created significant rockslides in the county and was a record breaker—a veritable 100-year flood. I didn't need to read about it in the paper to know.

✳ ✳ ✳

Survival Is All In Your Perspective

"The rivers in this area boast a lot of crocodiles. You must be wary if you are trying to get a picture of them. They move faster than you'd think," said the older Costa Rican gentleman who was driving the van. Carlos was a native who ran his own shuttle service between the airport in San Jose and various jungle locales around Costa Rica. I was going to rendezvous with some friends in the town of Quepos, a few hours to the south, for a few days of jungle training. As we drove over the cement two-lane bridge, he pointed a leathery finger to his right at a cluster of fifteen or so crocs sunning themselves along a tar-colored embankment.

I had just arrived in Costa Rica the day before and heard the tragic reports of a 7.0 earthquake that rocked Haiti. The news was filled with the graphic images of rubble and devastation. More than a few people in San Jose were concerned that such a quake could strike their own country. In the confined space of the dilapidated van, I could hear a trio of three buddies, who were headed to Jaco to surf, discussing what they would do if a similar disaster crippled Costa Rica and they were stranded long-term. Their plans played out like a scripted reality show and distracted me from enjoying the countryside outside my window. One of the guys said he would head to the coast, pull out a wad of cash and hire a boat to take him up to Panama, then walk back to the United States. The clean-cut guy next to him said he would stay in town and live with the locals, lounging in his hammock while whiling away the months in a margarita-filled haze. The third fellow, with a patchy five-o'clock shadow, mentioned he would simply disappear into the jungle. There he would feast on monkeys and toucans while wrestling a living from the bush with a machete. Then when things had returned to normal, he would emerge in his loincloth and venture back to civilization twenty pounds heavier.

Carlos asked politely if any of them had ever used a machete, after which they all shook their heads in the negative. The older man went on to describe his younger days when he and his father would head into the palm groves to cut timber and live off the jungle for weeks. His massive shovel-like hands, with scars peppering his knuckles, were a testament to a hard life out on the land.

He spoke in a soft tone, discussing encounters with poisonous snakes, crocodiles, and torrential storms. Carlos said he was only driving the shuttle van for a few months to pay off some of his daughter's medical bills before returning to the small town where he grew up.

The van was silent after he spoke as we took in the emerald mountains around us while winding along the narrow blacktop road. After we dropped the young men off at their destination, we continued on to Quepos. I sat in the seat next to Carlos, who was happy to play tour guide, pointing out the natural features along the verdant route ahead. I thought back on the dialogue that had played out earlier and asked the man what he would do if such an earthquake struck his country and completely devastated the region. Would he retreat to the hills that he knew so well? He smiled again and replied with a heavy accent, "I would make my way to my sister's town by the ocean and spend my days fishing for food. As long as a man can eat well and sleep well with his family by his side there is little else to worry about in life."

A few hours later, he dropped me off at my destination and we said adios. I think often about his words and the confidence that rolled off his tongue borne from a life out on the land with a minimum of gear and plenty of know-how.

* * *
Cold

During the winter of 1989, I had the good fortune of working as a co-instructor for a wilderness youth rehab program based out of southern Idaho, originally started by legendary instructor Larry Dean Olsen. This was my second 21-day survival trip after my initial apprenticeship earlier in the fall. I had heard stories about the desert being just as unforgiving in the winter as the summer but had no idea until this trip.

After picking up our students in Boise, we drove out to the desert region north of Bliss. This area is on the cusp of the northern edge of the Great Basin Desert. The land is comprised of seemingly endless mesas lined with giant sagebrush, with the Soldier Mountains serving as a backstop to the north.

The garb that we were permitted to carry was sparse: four upper body layers consisting of a t-shirt, flannel shirt, sweatshirt, and wool sweater; two lower body layers of long underwear and wool pants; a wool cap and mittens along with Sorel Pac boots completed the outfit. No down jackets, parkas, sleeping bags, or tents were allowed by the director, and we were told to use our wool blanket and army poncho as a shawl to stay warm. This was to prove a considerable challenge as the temperature rarely rose above ten degrees and our food intake hovered around 1200 calories a day. Still, I was in my early 20s and up for anything, not to mention being smitten with the desert. Heck, I would've done those trips for free just for the experience. However, in later years, I was reminded that good judgment comes from experience and most of that comes from bad judgment. Little did any of us know what was about to head our way during the middle of that three-week outing.

We spent the first four days centered around an immense underground lava tube where we taught primitive skills, trapped rodents, and mostly choked on campfire smoke given the poor ventilation conditions in the cave. Just when we'd had enough coughing, we'd venture up top where Mother Nature would quickly provide instruction in hypothermia and frostbite, but at least the wind cleared up our bloodshot eyes momentarily. Alternating between our subterranean chamber of smoldering sagebrush and the wind-chilled plateau helped me understand better why our ancestors only lived to twenty-five.

Food was simple and consisted of one cup per person of rice, lentils, oats, raisins, brown sugar, and flour. This was to last each of us for one week so everyone was highly motivated to become proficient at trapping and hunting.

Our co-ed group consisted of five youth from various parts of the country. They were required to spend three weeks with us in the desert as part of their overall ten-week substance abuse recovery program in Seattle. Back then, the parents weren't involved much in the program and they viewed us as mechanics that would "fix" their kids and send them back home with a new outlook on life. When we met the parents at the trail's end on day 21, it quickly became apparent that they perhaps played the biggest role in the destructive behavior of their children. The majority of the families were from the Silicon Valley area and many of the kids would describe their opulent lifestyles, while their parents' affection rarely factored into their conversations. One sixteen-year-old student even had his own Porsche and a separate house across from his parents' estate.

Nowadays, wilderness rehab programs recognize how essential parental involvement is in the overall outcome but during the infancy of these programs the approach mostly involved thrusting adolescents into the wilds and letting their grueling ordeal facilitate their road to recovery. In many cases, this worked, but I only saw the narrow window of time that we had them on the trail. I wondered what happened to them and their newfound self-esteem when they returned home to the same setting, parental issues, and peer group that led to the damaging behavior in the first place.

I do know that in all the wilderness programs I have worked over the years, the 21-day survival experience was remarkable for reshaping people's attitude towards themselves and what they were capable of. I can recall many students who arrived with such low self-esteem that they wouldn't look anyone in the eye and had their shoulders slumped forward. Often by day ten, this had changed remarkably as they realized, maybe for the first time in their lives, that they could take control of their destiny and shape their own outcomes through sheer persistence. The desert was a huge asset of course, as Mother Nature provided immediate feedback on whether a student had to work more on their skills. There was no blame game for the students to play with the other participants. Either you got your fire and shelter built or you were in for a miserable night.

We had a requirement that each student had to make their own fire every day, using flint and steel or the bow-drill method. As this was the only way to boil water to cook the rice and lentil meal, participants became extremely motivated after one night of hunger.

On this particular winter trip, we spent the first part of the week in the lava tubes and then snowshoed cross-country 8-10 miles a day to different cowboy line shacks dotting the desert wilderness. These were crude structures about the size of a 12'x14' shed with a small woodstove. One we stayed in was an underground root cellar and we had a hard time convincing ourselves to leave that snug abode. With daylight averaging only eight hours, we jammed instruction, hiking, navigation, and plenty of firewood collecting into that timeframe. Again, all of this was done on around 1200 calories a day and I ended up losing a considerable amount of bodyweight towards the end despite procuring the occasional rabbit or squirrel.

Life fell into a rhythm as it often does on the trail and everything was proceeding on track until day ten. On that blustery morning, we were instructed by our field director, via our daily radio check-in, to pack up from the cozy root cellar and proceed eight miles to a line-shack below the rim. Our meager food supply was running low and we would be out completely that evening. We hoped to have some luck with trapping a new area, and our director would drop by for his weekly visit in his snow-cat to resupply us with rations and whatever critter he shot along the way.

We set out after a meager breakfast on the long snowshoe trek. Walking in a single-file line not far from the mesa's edge, we traversed the monotonous white terrain and arrived at our destination around noon. After counting the miles until we would be out of the stinging cold, our tiny band crested the edge and saw a dilapidated cowboy shack below. It was around fifteen feet in diameter and had nylon tarps nailed onto three walls, which were flapping violently in the wind. I couldn't tell if it was the cold at that point, but the color drained out of most people's faces at the grim sight of our new home.

We descended and entered the hexagonal structure. After clearing away some old rat nests, we got the stove fired up with wet firewood stacked outside. My co-instructor, Joe, and I settled into teaching a module on first aid but, with spirits so low and energy levels waning, we would've been better off snoozing.

That night at dinner we pooled our scant supplies into one pot and shared the rice and lentil gruel. Then everyone set their deadfall traps around the perimeter of the shack and settled into their single blankets on the wooden floor. I remember waking up around midnight to an ominous sensation that had descended upon the shack. The air itself felt like a giant hand was pressing down on us and the wind had increased, jerking the flimsy tarp walls. A few other people sat up at the same time and we all traded disconcerted looks around the glow of the crackling woodstove.

The next morning, with a growling stomach, I trekked up to the ridge of the mesa to radio out for our daily check. The wind was ferocious, and despite my layers, felt like it was stabbing through my core. In a shaky voice, the field director informed us that an Arctic storm had swept in from the north, plummeting the temperature 48 degrees in one hour last night. The forecast indicated a "high" of -35 for the next few days. He told us we needed to get out of the region immediately before the coming snowfall made the area impassable.

After relaying the urgent need for departure to the group, we quickly assembled our wool blanketpacks, donned our snowshoes, and headed back up to the mesa. Our hunger pangs matched the fury of the icy wind as we crested the ridge. My depleted body struggled with each step and my mind kept racing ahead to the snug root cellar eight miles distant that awaited us. We walked in single file a few hundred feet from the rim of the mesa, trudging along in our snowshoes at a pace that was half of what it had been the day before along this same route.

The landscape was so monotonously white in every direction that there was little else to focus on except the heels of the person in front of me. About a mile in, with the wind chill hovering around -40, I had a strange sensation in my arms and legs that I had never before experienced. It was a very organic sensation—of my life force draining from my extremities and retreating into my core. My limbs weren't numb from frostbite (not yet anyway). It reminded me of the survival mechanism a desert tree initiates during a drought when it sacrifices a limb to save the trunk. I forced my legs to move forward with each punishing step in the crusty, windswept snow. I felt again, this time more pronounced, the energy trickling out of my extremities and into the center of my chest. My heart raced with concern and I felt like my entire being was reduced to a delicate flicker that I had to keep alive at all costs. I was too drained and mentally spent to realize I was coping with hypothermia and potential frostbite.

I recall stopping around mile six alongside some boulders and checking on the group. Everyone had the same glazed look in their eyes, which were bordered below by pasty cheeks. After doing a safety check on each person to make sure they could still feel their fingers and toes, everyone chugged down some nearly frozen water from their canteens and replaced it with fresh snow. I could hear myself speaking but it sounded disconnected, like a robot was pushing out the words from my lips. I could still sense my own extremities but my legs felt like they were stuck in quicksand with each movement.

As we headed away from the ridge towards a low-lying sagebrush forest in the distance, I felt the energy drain further from me as I fought to keep that shrinking flicker in my chest from going out completely. I can still remember looking down at my stick legs and being shocked at how thin they had become from drastic weight loss (over twenty pounds by trip's end). My body had been feeding on its lean muscle mass to provide fuel for the past week and now the extreme temperature drop was probably thrusting that evolutionary mechanism into high gear.

I kept envisioning the light in my chest as all that was left of me—I had to keep the flame aglow no matter how hard it was to walk. I had to help Joe get the group back to the shelter. Each step became a workout in willpower and a part of me just wanted to lie down and stop fighting the wind.

Seven hours after we had begun our trek, we arrived at the underground root cellar. This was double the amount of time it had taken us previously hiking to the other structure. Descending the creaky plank board steps, our weary, hypothermic group filled the 12'x15' earthen shelter. After firing up the woodstove, I checked on the other students to make sure no one had frostbite and then I collapsed in the corner. The snug dwelling warmed quickly but it did little to restore my body's core temperature. We went without food that night and it wasn't until later the next afternoon that our field director arrived in his snow-cat. We had lost radio contact with him during that time due to the storm and he probably wasn't sure what kind of scene he would be walking into when he clamored down the stairs.

What I remember most about his arrival was the assortment of food he brought—a stack of bananas, peanut butter, yogurt, lunchmeat, and canned fruit along with resupplying our usual rations. I consumed an entire jar of peanut butter and a can of pears within minutes, greedily scooping out the contents with a thin slab of cottonwood. We spent the remaining four days at that root cellar, glad to be out of the wind, but I was ready for the warmth of the sun and my own space. For the remainder of the trip, I found it impossible to get warm no matter how hot the woodstove blazed or how many layers I donned.

After the trip ended, I retreated to the instructor trailer in Bliss for a few days of rest. I ended up sleeping for 56 hours, only managing to get up to have the occasional drink of water or choke down a cold slice of pizza. I had some time off during the winter and flew back to Michigan to visit with my family. It took me another two months before my body recovered its ability to properly thermoregulate. All I recall from that time off was consuming endless amounts of pasta, milkshakes, and slabs of meat while my parents constantly frowned at my ravenous appetite (and their dreadful grocery bills). I've since decided that winter trips are best enjoyed with copious amounts of food, a parka, a down sleeping bag, infinite amounts of hot chocolate, and a weather radio.

* * *

A Five Scorpion Night

James was a seventeen-year veteran of the special operations community whose unit we had provided survival training for over the years. He was a sinewy warrior who moved like a cat. This time out, he and three of his fellow team members came on an advanced course that we put on in the high desert tailored to their specific training needs.

The timeframe was four days and I was informed that they only wanted to take ten pounds of gear consisting mostly of clothes and a few survival items. Given that we were in the desert in the spring time, water weight was not included. A 2-way radio, topographic map, compass, and knife were also excluded from the weight tally as these guys had done plenty of bare-bones courses using improvised tools before.

All four men came dressed in their usual fatigues, desert boots, shemagh, and boonie hat. Each carried a Camelbak with a 2-liter water supply. Inside the pack were several undergarments, fleece jacket, Iodine tablets, spark rod, and a one-ounce bottle of Tabasco. They were then given the choice of taking either extra food or extra clothing. Three of them chose to bring an MRE each. James, who was an experienced hunter, opted to skip the food and bring more clothing instead.

The morning class was a refresher on edible plants, hazardous creatures, water location strategies, and safety protocols in the event of a medical emergency. Afterwards, we drove the four men north of our basecamp and dropped them off in separate locations with instructions to call in twice a day with their position. They could either do a long trek of ten miles that first day to the coordinates I provided and stay in one camp the remainder of the course, or spread their mileage out each day, making new camps along the way.

After giving each man the coordinates of where they needed to end up, they disappeared into the windy sagebrush flats of the mesa. Meanwhile, my instructors and I drove back to our basecamp. Every morning and evening, each man did a radio check-in to make sure they were staying hydrated and to just do a general assessment of how they were holding up. It was a pretty warm spring at our location, with daytime temps in the 80 degree range and nighttime temps hovering around 40 degrees. The only problem was that the unceasing winds made having a small campfire for cooking or warmth out of the question.

As the information on the radio-checks was minimal and mainly related to medical assessments, we didn't hear much about the day-to-day adventures until after the course ended. It wasn't until the evening of day four, when we were out of the field having a beer with all of the guys, that we got to hear the gritty details of how each man fared.

Out of the many things I admire about the special operations guys is the attitude of success they have built into every undertaking. That saying, "Failure is not an option" is something that is akin to a religious mantra to these men and no matter how hard, how far, how difficult the task, they are utterly determined to get the job done regardless of the adversity ahead. James' food procurement strategies were no exception and his quest to quell hunger drove him towards a unique solution.

The first night, James didn't have any luck locating wild foods like cattails or in obtaining a jackrabbit. Then he recalled how an earlier lecture had mentioned that eighty percent of the desert's biomass came from insects and other creepy crawlies. Waiting until the sun set, he grabbed a four-foot springy sapling of willow and began flipping over rocks in the arroyo below his camp. Within minutes he had skewered a few scorpions and carried them back to his abode. After lopping off the stingers, he then pulverized the crème-colored critters on a slab of sandstone and choked down the crunchy gruel. The second night saw the consumption of only three scorpions. On the last night, James said he obtained five large scorpions but rather than mashing them into the usual, boring arthropod paste, he used a fuel tablet from his survival kit to roast the batch of five critters. Then he dabbed each crusty carapace with several drops of precious Tabasco that he had saved for the last night.

"Now that was some fine dining, the likes of which you other fellas will never know," he said, rolling a toothpick between his lips while a grin crept out.

* * *

KUYI

In the Great Lakes where I grew up, we had a saying that Fire is Life, but here in the arid Southwest, your day revolves around water. Water creates its own desires in the mind of a thirsty man. It's no wonder that water-related petroglyphs abound in so many desert regions. In such an unforgiving land, you quickly become a hunter of shade for a part of each day and seriously ponder how much a given activity will cost you in sweat.

When two backcountry guides get together in downtown Flagstaff, you'll often hear every other sentence peppered with, "How much water did you go through on that trip?" or "Were there any reliable springs along that trail?" or "Did you find any decent cattle troughs along the way?"

While poring over a new topographic map of an area to explore, my eyes always float over the contour lines in search of water sources before anything else. Here in the Southwest, we have many names for agua: tinajas, seeps, springs, water pockets, stock tanks, cowholes, rain basins. Often where I locate water, I will scan the rocks overhead and find rock art because the ancients had their villages, trade routes, and clan meeting sites wherever reliable water was found.

The Hopi have a word that translates into a saying in our culture—*Paatuwaqatsi* or "Water is Life." Kuyi is another Hopi term that means water and, not surprisingly, KUYI is also the name for the Hopi radio station at Keams Canyon, east of the village of Second Mesa. I remember some of my older Hopi friends telling me about how when they were teenagers, the fun thing to do was to run barefoot from the village at Second Mesa to the town of Winslow to watch the arrival of the afternoon train. Then they would run back home. That's a distance of over a hundred miles roundtrip and they weren't carrying daypacks full of water bottles or wearing Nikes. They knew the location of the seeps, springs, and water caches that had been used by countless generations of travelers in that windswept region. Water is life.

When June rolls around in the Southwest and the air feels like a blast furnace, a backcountry explorer appreciates water on a deep cellular level. On desert survival courses that I have taught to special operations groups, we are sometimes out in 112+ degree heat for a week and easily sucking down 3-4 gallons of water per person per day. After a while, you start to feel like a two-legged waterfall.

Under such conditions, electrolyte replacement is critical, as too much water begins to dilute the electrolytes in your bloodstream and you can succumb to hyponatremia or water intoxication, something that afflicts many hikers in the Grand Canyon. For every sixty minutes of strenuous activity in the intense heat, we take a mandatory shade break, rehydrate with half a liter of water or more, and suck down some type of electrolyte replacement fluids like Hydralyte or GU20. Pretzels, salty nuts, and bananas are what my ranching friends use but they are too bulky in my daypack.

Strangers to the desert often think that they can obtain water from any nearby cactus because they saw the surly hero in a Western movie do it. In reality, there is only one cactus—the fishhook barrel—and I would hardly call the nasty, viscous, glue-like goo extracted from its innards water. It is high in alkaloids and has a considerable gag factor too, so don't plan on quenching your thirst from one; plus there are four other barrel cacti that are toxic lookalikes. The few times I have tried choking down barrel cactus fluid I felt my stomach churn like a cement mixer. There's a reason cactus juice is not sold on the shelves at the grocery store! Yet, this method still shows up in Hollywood movies, reality shows, and magazine articles on desert survival.

The other most common misconception is the notion of using a solar still for procuring water in the desert. Whenever I glance through a new survival book, I always check to see what the author has written about the solar still. If they say it's an effective means of procuring water in arid regions, then I place the book back on the shelf.

On every desert survival course, we construct a solar still just to show the futility of this method. After digging a 3' deep hole that is 3' in diameter (and we all carry shovels in our packs, right?), we line the pit with succulent cacti to boost the output, place a cup in the bottom and then seal it up with an inverted 6'x6' sheet of clear plastic. We even intentionally construct the still in the damp soil of an arroyo or canyon floor that has recently seen rain. The next day, after the still has had 24 hours to work, we pull back the plastic cover and voila—there's about a half quart of clear fluid! Wow! Then we remember back to the previous day when we burned off a gallon of sweat making the still.

Unfortunately for the general public, barrel cacti and solar stills show up way too often in the media as key methods for obtaining water. The single best method I know for staying hydrated in the wilderness is to be prepared and carry water with you, especially in the desert, where there isn't any water for much of the year (hmm…that's why it's called a desert). The most reliable water source is your faucet at home because you planned ahead. If you do chance across some agua in the backcountry, consider yourself blessed as the ancient travelers did, and give thanks for this precious substance that makes life possible. Without it, you'd become jerky.

While I always encourage students to purify suspect water sources in the backcountry, I didn't always have the luxury of adhering to such advice. During a three-week survival trek in the desert, we found all of our usual waterholes dried up from a longstanding drought. On day six we crested a place called Deer Heaven Mesa and swigged down the last of the water from our canteens. The sixteen-mile hike had worn everyone out and a few quarts of cold spring water would have gone a long way to replenishing our spent bodies. As we surveyed the area below, one student shouted with joy to a distant body of water that was shimmering in the fading sunlight. It was about two miles away from the bottom of the mesa. We would have to wait until sunrise to immerse our dusty faces in that delightful basin.

Everyone was half-hydrated and we went to sleep that night without eating to cut down on further loss of bodily fluid. If you don't have water, you shouldn't eat, unless you've got a pack full of apples. Besides, there was no way to cook our usual fare of rice and lentils so cottonmouths and empty stomachs were the only menu items available.

That night, as we all lay on grass mats within the fragrant stands of sagebrush, everyone began talking about water in its different forms: rivers, oceans, swimming pools, waterfalls, ice cubes, lemon water, carbonated water, shaved ice, and snow. From fishing trips to beach parties to snowball fights, everyone began muttering tales spurred by longing and parched throats. It was amazing what deprivation of something so primal does to a group's storytelling ability! As I fell asleep staring up at the Big Dipper, my head ached slightly from the early stages of dehydration and I forced myself to focus on the memory of that glimmering waterhole we had spied earlier. That lusty image kept re-emerging throughout my sagebrush-scented slumber.

A few magpies awoke us at dawn and we hastily packed our blankets into packs and gathered our remaining gear. Everyone was sluggish from dehydration but there were no forced smiles that morning as we each looked down below the mesa at the treasure awaiting us.

With hollow canteens clanking against our sides, we eagerly descended the rim like a group of kids at Halloween rushing to a porch-light. The students began talking about which one would dunk their head in first and imbibe a mouthful of cold spring water, and what it would taste like, as if the memory of such daily undertakings had already been erased. With only a few hundred yards to go, we plowed through the sagebrush, following a well-worn trail, all the time keeping the ever-growing reflection from the waterhole in our crosshairs. *How did it get there? Is it natural—a spring perhaps? Or is it maintained by the ranchers in the area? How deep is it? Maybe we can go for a swim after our thirst is slaked.* All these thoughts ran through my head as my pace quickened and my parched lips continued cracking with each crooked smile of the pleasure that was to come.

As we emerged from the thicket of sagebrush, the waterhole was before us. We felt like explorers emerging into a new world, like greedy prospectors who had stumbled upon a precious vein of undiscovered gold; and then it happened—we were suddenly stopped in our tracks by a smothering odor. It was an odd blend of cowpies, animal urine, and moldy earth. As I pulled my bandanna up around my nose, I glanced over at our cauldron of salvation in the ground and saw flies hovering over the algae-coated surface of a coffee-colored basin. Upon moving closer, I saw the mud covered in fresh cow tracks and disheveled rows of submerged cowpies that resembled underwater buttes. A few feet from the edge of the frothy cesspool, some unknown type of white, ribbon-like worm wriggled through the slick black water and disappeared into the murky liquid.

We looked at each other with gaunt expressions, our red cheeks sinking in further from the dwindling fluid within our own bodies. I had seen that look before in others and knew the feeling in myself all too well. That cellular urge for water that became so great you would push someone out of the way for a drink, no matter how foul the source. We withdrew a few feet away under the shade of a large cottonwood tree and pored over the topographic map. The nearest springs were about six miles away, if they were there at all with the current drought. This was our only reliable water source. Several students were already getting lightheaded and we wouldn't have the luxury of boiling water and letting it cool in the desert heat. I urged the group to follow me back to the "waterhole." Dropping down on my chest, I lowered my face and issued the advice given to me by an old cowboy: "Just grit your teeth to strain out the big stuff." Then, I closed my eyes and slurped up a few quarts off the surface, the tepid brown sludge sliding past my chapped lips.

After everyone filled their bellies, we moved back under the shade of the cottonwood and built a small fire. We spent the next hour boiling water from the cowhole to replenish our canteens before hiking on to our next camp six miles distant. We had to use that cowboy method one other time on that trip as our usual water sources had dried up. Amazingly nobody suffered any ill-effects, though for some time, it sounded like our stomachs were rumbling like race cars and very few animals were spotted downwind of our group.

* * *
The Cave Where Tom Lived

Students in my courses often ask if there are any more actual mountain men living in the wilds today. I know of a few guys but their lifestyle is more of a melding of modern and pioneer skills. One friend lives nine miles down a gnarly jeep trail in an off-grid homestead, only coming into town once every three months. Another dwells part-time in a handmade pithouse and wears buckskin obtained from deer he procures with an atlatl and obsidian-tipped spear points.

Most of the others are living relatively untethered between worlds—they come into town several times a week or each month to get some supplies, check their mail (and in one case, email!), and visit a bookstore. The majority are guys that are true hermits, simply wanting to be left alone in their wilderness sanctuaries. Some like the freedom that comes with rent-free living in the forest coupled with excursions into town to visit friends and grab the occasional cup of coffee.

I know of one such individual in Flagstaff, whose name is Tom, and he has been living a Spartan existence in a cave for the past eighteen years. I visited his abode once after a rock-climbing buddy showed me the location. It was a cave that took some effort to get to with all of the cactus and yucca lining the arroyo below it. That's probably what kept his location secure for so long—that and the fact that he was such a good steward of the area.

When I worked for the Forest Service years ago, we would occasionally come across squatters living out of their vans in the backcountry. You could see their encampments from a mile off as they had accumulated months of trash along with denuding every tree in the region for firewood. Not Tom, though—this sixty-eight-year-old fellow has been an exemplary caretaker of his "backyard" and has even saved lost hikers over the years. I had to literally walk up on his cave before I knew there was someone living there, so unobtrusive was his location. The ironic thing was that he lived in an area that was a ten-minute walk from an upscale neighborhood that butted against the mountains.

If you run into Tom on the streets of Flagstaff, you'd think he was a college professor given his trim silver beard, stylish beret, and sprightly walk. He's also involved in local politics! Before he was evicted from his first cave by the authorities, he had simple digs. His dwelling was about ten feet deep. It was complete with a bookshelf, coat-rack, tiny fire pit, and a sleeping area that had a shower curtain to keep out the elements. Anyone who can make it through years of Flagstaff winters in a cave is a tough hombre. He wasn't living off the land but would come into town once a week to work odd jobs for cash to obtain food like rice, beans, veggies, and fruit.

When the authorities finally pinpointed his home, after years of fruitless searching, they told him to pack up a few belongings and leave. Tom replied, "Well, I guess it's time for me simplify my life anyway."

His eviction caused quite a stir in town as many locals knew where he lived and recalled what a fine caretaker he had been. When I spoke with the reporter who covered the story, he said that over ninety media outlets from around the world had called the newspaper wanting an interview with the mountain man but Tom had refused. The reporter also told me that when a background search was done, nothing turned up other than that Tom had dodged the Vietnam draft. In this modern era, it's astounding that no other information exists on the man.

Two weeks later, I saw him walking up the trail towards the mountains and he has been there ever since. I suspect, as with most long-term wilderness dwellers seeking to remain low profile, he now has several caves that he rotates through during the month and is at a higher elevation to avoid running into hikers. He probably knows that mountain ecosystem better than anyone since the days of the Anasazi Indians and I'm sure he could fill a book with stories on all of his wildlife encounters.

* * *

Gramps

The dog that staggered into our desert camp in early November was an old-timer, his ribs showing through his paper-thin hide and his far-off gaze indicative of dehydration. He looked like a sauntering skeleton with fur, and he had been holding on to life by a thread. With water so scarce, and with the concentration of coyote packs in the region that fall, it was amazing he'd made it at all.

Perhaps it was the dog's size that had helped. He looked like a bulldog/mastiff mix with a white-mottled caramel coat. His bear-like head revealed serene blue eyes and he had a heart to match his size. Gentle and sweet-natured, he sat calmly but with an upward gaze of anticipation, like a dog who's used to seeing meat-flavored treats shoot out of his owner's pockets.

He appeared two days before the start of a 21-day bushcraft course at our basecamp near the Painted Desert. Two work-study students from abroad, Carmen and Matt, were with me, helping to set up camp. It was Matt who noticed the dog first as it stumbled past the dirt road over to our outdoor kitchen. Carmen playfully called the weathered canine *Gramps* and the name stuck.

I gave him water and a bowl of food, from my own dog's stash in the truck, and after gorging himself on both, he collapsed in a heap under the shade of a juniper for about four hours. His snoring was so obnoxious it even kept the local ravens from pestering us. In fact, as we were to find out, snoring was something he excelled at. Even when we sat around the evening campfire, he would plunk down beside us and let his canine chainsaw roar. If you were talking, you'd have to raise your voice a level to overcome Gramps' bellowing. And if you couldn't find Gramps around camp, all that was needed was to be silent for a moment and his slumbering nasal bugle would betray his location under the shade of a nearby tree. His snuffling became quite a comical attribute, so much so that when someone had slept well, they'd say, "Man, I slept as hard as Gramps last night." We surmised that sleeping and snoring were the dog's two favorite activities.

In the days that followed his arrival, I spent some time asking other families spread around the valley if they recognized the dog, but to no avail. For the time being, he became our camp mascot. Early on, he was taken in by Matt, who was Gramps' first target for sympathy. Matt was residing in a large canvas pyramid tent and the lumbering bulldog, not liking to sleep alone, didn't think a closed doorway was any way to treat a tired friend. He would blast through the entrance, shaking the tent as he entered, and then plop down next to, or on top of, Matt. And then the snoring festival would begin. Matt's caffeine intake increased as the days went by.

Upon waking each morning and plowing out of Matt's tent, Gramps would walk around camp looking for the rest of his human tribe. For those still asleep on the bare ground, with only their faces showing through their bedrolls, he would deliver a slobbering kiss like the person's head was a big postage stamp. My co-instructor, Billy, received the brunt of these greetings and his sunrise cussing served as an alarm that Gramps was on the prowl.

The first week of the course was focused on the basic skills of bushcraft such as firemaking, shelters, survival kits, carving skills, tracking, and edible plants to name a few. Week two emphasized hide tanning, using the traditional method of brain tanning. During this phase, most everyone wanted to make a sleeveless shirt, which required two softened, braintanned deer hides. It was arm-wrenching work, and it took roughly two days to completely tan one hide, if all the steps were correctly followed.

I had an arrangement with a local game-processing shop in town that saved deer hides for us during hunting season, and we had a few dozen to work with when week two began. Most hunters today, when they field-dress a deer, aren't concerned with keeping the hide so the butchering job in the field is pretty crude. As a result, most hides have numerous slabs of steak on them. However, Gramps was grateful.

That week, we were standing over our individual tanning posts scraping chunks of fat and meat off the hides when Gramps showed up with the look of a dog who had clearly wandered into venison heaven.

At first he stood by the scraping posts with a mesmerized gaze. A second later, Matt, who was holding up a 6" slab of meat by the now-drooling dog, asked, "Do you think it's OK for Gramps to…." Before he could finish, Gramps slurped down the glistening patty like it was a spaghetti noodle. Then he proceeded to clean up the rest of the meat scraps on the ground. "Uhm…I guess it's OK!" said Matt.

By the end of that day, Gramps must have eaten about 12 pounds of raw venison. By week's end, he had filled out nicely and hardly seemed like the same gaunt creature that had showed up earlier. Of course, his snoring never improved and only seemed to increase in volume with his satisfied belly. Near the end of week two, I told my wife that we might have another dog joining our pack at home. Gramps got along great with my kids whenever they came out to visit and his sweet nature made for an easy friend. We already had four dogs that we'd rescued over the years so finding his original owners was high on my list.

Still, week three entailed us leaving on a 7-day walkabout and I was worried that Gramps might not stay close to the group while on the trail. I feared he might end up lost all over again in a very rugged wilderness area. As I was heading to town the day before we left for the walkabout, I tried one last time to locate his owners. I posted another sign several miles down the road on a wooden billboard by the main entrance to the area.

That night, I got a call from a young woman named Lindsey, inquiring about Gramps. She said that she and her family had recently moved to the area from California and that their cherished dog had gotten out three weeks ago. My description matched hers and I told her to meet me by the entrance to the property the next morning and I would guide her into our camp.

The following day, I drove out to meet Lindsey, who had her two young daughters along. She followed me in her weathered blue pickup as we drove through groves of familiar juniper trees and along the dusty, winding roads to our remote camp. Upon arriving, I got out of my rig and shouted for Gramps. Everyone was waiting by the vehicles and had their gear packed for our trip. The air was filled with anticipation from both parties. Lindsey and her little girls were tense, hoping it was their long-lost pooch, and my students were hoping that Gramps wouldn't leave our little tribe.

I called again for the old timer and he came lumbering up from a thicket of trees where he'd been asleep. Lindsey and the girls' eyes widened at his approach. They ran forward with excitement shouting, "It's him—it's Junior!" Lindsey and her tots threw themselves onto the dog as he slathered them with that rug-sized tongue while rolling in the dirt with glee. There wasn't a dry eye in camp. A family was reunited but there were also farewells to be said.

A few minutes and many smiles later, Lindsey turned and heard me mumbling, "Huh, Junior? You gotta be kidding—this old timer?" Lindsey stood up while her dog pressed against her leg. *"Junior* is a purebred American Bulldog that we got from a breeder when he was eight months old. He's my third baby in the family and is only a year old."

Time was at a brief standstill as we all bade them adios and watched the family drive off with Gramps-Junior hanging his cappuccino-colored head out the truck's window. The eight of us stood still, with misty eyes, waving to our four-legged pal like we were parents ushering a child off on the first day of school.

It was time to pack up and head off on our trip. During the rest of the week in the forest, our campfire tales centered not around the lofty vistas, foraged meals, or our daily trials but around our old canine compadre. He will forever be known as Gramps to those of us who had the good fortune to meet him and partake of his antics, snoring, and charm.

Lindsey and her family have moved on, but the memory of Gramps lingers at our camp and I recount his tale often around the woodsmoke of the campfire. I sometimes wonder if he thinks of his adopted desert tribe and his venison-filled days, and if he remembers us the way we remember him. Though he was only with us for a few weeks, I'll never forget that dog.

Live long and snore prosperously, Gramps!

* * *
A Tale Of Two Countries

"I've been to nearly 43 countries in the world. I just can't get enough of seeing this beautiful globe," said Gerald, a forty-three-year-old businessman who was riding shotgun in my Tacoma. We were enroute to Utah for a five-day fieldcourse that I was co-teaching with a friend.

Gerald had been on several other courses and I always enjoyed his cosmopolitan outlook on life given how much he had traveled during the past eleven years. He was one of seven other participants , the other two of which were riding in the back seat along with the rest in another vehicle behind us.

It was a four-hour drive through some of the finest scenery in the world. The Painted Desert, Monument Valley, and Comb Ridge lay ahead of us and we had many fine discussions on such drives. With the other two students lost in their own conversation, I grilled Gerald on his globetrotting adventures.

"The architecture in Dubai is outrageous and visionary. Nothing can compare to it," he said. "Though I did once stay in a bamboo skyscraper in Malaysia with monkeys waking us up on our balcony each morning," he said while constantly craning his head at the massive red buttes in the distance.

"Out of all of your travels, did you ever find the perfect getaway—a place that you'd return to and stay indefinitely?" I asked.

Without even taking a breath, he replied, "Tunisia…I would drop what I am doing now and zip back there if I could. I just loved Tunisia—the people, the cities, the cuisine. Man, that is one place I can't get enough of."

"Tunisia, eh…I'll have to file that one away," I said. "Sounds promising."

The rest of the drive alternated between Gerald sharing some far-flung trip and me narrating on the natural or native history of the Navajo lands we were passing through.

Later that morning, we arrived at the bunkhouse in a remote section of Utah. This would be our base for the duration of the course. For the next five days, the students learned what was involved in modern hunting and trapping, wild game processing, making jerky, tracking, and reading the landscape. It was an intensive hands-on course and everyone left with a better understanding of the realities of living off the land.

On the drive back to Flagstaff, participants switched around their locations in the vehicles and I had a new set of guys in my truck. Raymond, a brawny fellow who had been a Navy SEAL, sat in the passenger's seat and regaled us with more tales of his former experiences abroad on government-sponsored vacations. He had been to over 28 countries in either the SEALs or as a private contractor. As we crested a ridge overlooking the buttes of Monument Valley, I asked him what the worst country was that he had been to in his career.

"Tunisia, without a doubt! What a putrid rat-hole. Couldn't stand the culture, the cities, or the rancid food there. Man, I'd fling myself from a plane without a parachute before I'd go back there again."

* * *

Nightmare On Elm Creek

"I'd like to head off into the bush with only a blanket, knife, and some rice while harvesting everything else from the wilds. Can we set up such a primitive walkabout for sometime this fall?" said the gravelly voice of the man on the phone. His name was Carl and he spoke with an unusually calm, almost sedated voice. A recent *Backpacker* magazine article on my survival school had brought in a flurry of interest and Carl was eager to discuss a five-day trek into the desert to live off the land. He said he was a self-employed artist from back east who wanted to take a break from the monotony of his work.

We made the arrangements for October. When the time came, I picked him up at the Greyhound station in Flagstaff and we headed out to the desert. Our gear was austere, as is typical for a primitive walkabout, and consisted of a wool blanket, poncho, knife, 64-ounce cooking pot, water bottle, Iodine tablets, 20' of para-cord, and the clothes on our back. Food was intentionally simple and involved a cup each of rice, lentils, flour, oats, raisins, and brown sugar. This was enough to sustain a person but also motivated you to forage and fish.

After an hour's drive, we hit the trail and made our way along the boulder-strewn pathway that led into a shallow canyon that had a beautiful creek flowing through it. The cottonwoods and sycamores were still lush with foliage and created the image of a green ribbon running along the canyon floor. Along the way, I spoke to Carl about the ancient Anasazi who lived here a thousand years ago and their survival strategies. Halfway in, we came across a small petroglyph panel with serpentine images and shapes that resembled half-human, half-animal figures.

While the hike to our proposed camp was only four miles, it took hours to reach it because Carl kept stopping to meditate on the scenery. The region is stunning but I constantly informed him that we had a lot of physical chores ahead of us if we were to stay warm, dry, hydrated, and fed. However, his attention was elsewhere and my admonitions largely went unnoticed. It was going to be a long night if we didn't gather enough firewood and construct our shelters before sundown. Eventually, after much prodding, we finally made it to a rock outcropping above the stream that I had used before. It was around twelve feet wide by twenty feet long with a jutting overhang which would provide much-needed shade over the coming days.

The region was exceptionally lush, with prickly pear cacti and yucca fruits sprinkled along the cliff faces. After dropping my blanketpack, I noticed the unusual amounts of rodent tracks in the sand. I informed Carl that we would have to be careful with food scraps or we'd be overrun by packrats and mice. The summer monsoons had been very productive which in turn had provided a spike in the animal population in the area. We went down to the creek and I discussed water purification. After refilling our water bottles, we focused on gathering armloads of downed cottonwood limbs and preparing grass mats for sleeping on. By the time we returned to our campsite, rodents had already chewed through our blanketpacks to extract the food packs inside. They didn't pilfer much but their blatant assault made me realize just how thick the small critters were in this canyon.

After completing our grass mats, I covered bow-drill firemaking with the available sunlight. Carl got a fire started after a few attempts with a yucca fireboard and drill. Then I prepped the pot of rice and lentils over the fire and later tossed some large yucca fruits into the coals to bake. The setting sun washed over the canyon in orange and red fingers while the bustle of birdsong from wrens and mourning doves grew silent. The only noise was a slight breeze rustling over the trees below and the constant scurrying of tiny rodent feet moving along the ledge behind us.

While we sat around the campfire carving spoons and coal-burning bowls, I told a story about Geronimo and the Apache Campaign that had unfolded in the region. Carl was busy carving a hunk of sycamore while I alternated between cooking and storytelling. He remained silent most of the evening with only an occasional chuckle to indicate that he was present. This struck me as odd given the fact that there was little humor in the bloody tale of warfare that I was recounting. An hour later, with the rice and lentils done, I pulled the sooty pot off the fire and let it cool in the sand.

Working with your hands under open skies brews up a fierce appetite and we were both ready to dig in to our simple stew. Just as I was about to remind Carl about the rodent issues we would face if we were careless with crumbs, he moved forward and accidentally kicked over the pot, spilling rice and lentils all over our blankets.

My jaw was unhinged and the hunger pangs in my stomach were churning into coils of distress. I'm quite sure that, at that same moment, throngs of mice and packrats sat back on their haunches and grinned. Carl muffled out an apology as we attempted to salvage the meal while futilely wiping the sludge off our wool bedrolls. The whole time, I felt like there were dozens of tiny eyes peering down at us, wondering how long before our campfire would die down.

The gritty stew was divided up and eaten. An hour later, after inspecting my soiled blanket, I took off my boots and crawled into my bed atop the grass mat. Tossing the last log on the fire, I lay back and stared up at the beige ceiling of rock overhead, wondering if any sleep was in store during the long night ahead. Carl was about four feet away, close to the creekside, while my bed was butted against the back of the rock overhang.

With the fire illuminating the sandstone walls, we both dozed off. That was short-lived as the patter of paws running across my chest and legs soon commenced. Despite constant shimmying and cussing, they kept prodding for leftovers. Just when I thought I had scared them off, I would feel a wet nose pressing into my hair or ear. As the night crawled along, we were overrun by dozens of mice and packrats who were little affected by our constant thrashing. At one point in the middle of the night, in my delirium, I dreamt of a large brown rat sitting near the campfire, his tale flicking back and forth. He knew my name and kept mocking me, saying the rice was too crunchy. I remember wanting to punt him into the creek but he was too fast and managed to get away with my cooking pot wrapped in his clutches.

Though I had thought of relocating our camp, the terrain was too treacherous to move around in at night and we would only be indulging another group of rodents who hadn't yet tasted wool-enriched rice and lentils.

At some point before dawn, I fell into a coma-like sleep. I awoke a few hours later as the sun was climbing over the jagged rim of the canyon across from our campsite. Carl was standing with his back to me, gazing over the creek below. I propped myself up on one elbow and shook my tussled, rodent-inspected hair while eking out a yawn. After the first night afield on a trip, I always like to ask my students how their shelter system worked and what they would do to improve things the following night. I could already think of a few suggestions to hammer home to Carl but wanted to hear his thoughts first.

I sat up and reached for my boots while asking Carl if he had gotten any sleep. He slowly turned and looked at me while the sun backlit his shaggy mop of gray hair. "Not very well," he said with a solemn stare. "I had a dream that I stabbed you to death and threw your body in the creek."

I stopped tying my boot and craned my head towards him, wondering if I had woken up in a Stanley Kubrick film, the zoom lens upon my face with the organ music in the background. Carl stood there silently, the cracked lips behind his thick beard not revealing a trace of movement. I glanced down at his belt where his knife was in its sheath and wondered how long he had been standing near me as I slept. Before I could reply, he said, "I think there are some bad spirits in this canyon and I should leave."

I immediately hopped up with one boot on, clipped my knife onto my belt and replied, "Yeah, that sounds like a great idea. Let's pack up and head out of here!"

Without hesitation, he knelt down and began gathering his gear while I shook my head, thinking that maybe last night's rodent assault wasn't so bad after all. I wondered if Carl was on some prescription medication that he had failed to mention on his health form. Regardless, we were leaving the canyon and this trip into bizarro-land was about to be over!

I hastily packed up my bedroll and doused the ashes from the campfire while keeping Carl in my crosshairs the entire time. I was sure I could hear a lot of fat rodents snoring in the rock piles around me but my attention was focused on the seemingly unbalanced individual in front of me. Within minutes of breaking camp, we headed back along the trail we came in on. I made sure that Carl walked in front of me and at a distance. He was a different person on the return hike, smiling, laughing, and marveling at the picturesque cliffs. That four-mile trek felt like it took two days but we finally made it back to the vehicle with me silently swearing never to do a custom course again with a self-employed artist from the East Coast. Thankfully Carl slept on the way back which allowed me to keep both hands on the steering wheel. Upon arriving in Flagstaff, he asked to be dropped at the Greyhound bus station. I can't say I remember hitting too many red lights on the return drive.

After he departed, I went downtown and grabbed a burger and reflected on the bizarre events that had just been distilled into the past twenty-four hours. Now if you come on one of my courses, don't take it personally if I don't ask how you've slept and don't be alarmed at the two dogs I have beside me. They're the reason I sleep so peacefully and also why there are no rodent tracks around my shelter.

* * *
A Real Man

One of the pleasures of working with the military special operations community is all of the stories that the guys share around the evening campfire when we've finished the day's teachings.

We have one unit in particular that we have been working with for many years and the unit's NCO, Mike, shared a great tale with us involving a camping trip he went on with his 14-year-old daughter who he visits with each summer.

Mike had taken his daughter Ashley on a 3-day campout in the forests of Pennsylvania. One evening, he wanted to show her how to make fire by friction, using the bow-drill. He had cut down a cedar branch and used it for his fireboard and drill while securing a maple branch for the bow. Using his bootlace for the bowstring and a chunk of maple for the handhold, he created a primitive fire in mere minutes. His daughter sat entranced the whole time, watching her father's finesse with the ancient skill. When Mike was done, she immediately grabbed the primitive tools and looked them over, yearning to recreate fire as her father had. It was a proud moment for Mike. They spent the rest of the evening working on survival skills, carving spoons, and laughing about other trips together.

Fast forward two weeks to Ashley's birthday party at her mom and stepdad's house. Amidst a crowd of friends and family, Ashley's stepdad is ready to light a blaze in the backyard fire pit. He returns from the garage with a stack of newspaper, matches, and a can of lighter fluid. Ashley moves forward in disgust at her stepdad's materials and declared, "A real man can make a fire with his bare hands and some sticks. A real man doesn't need to use matches or a lighter!"

An awkward silence enshrouded the guests as a frostbitten expression slid over her stepdad's face. Ashley's mom quickly stepped in and plucked her daughter from the crowd while comforting her husband.

Later that night, Mike got a call from his daughter recounting the whole story and could barely restrain his laughter. However, Mike said his ex-wife had another take on the story and its long-lasting ripple effect at the party.

✳ ✳ ✳

Ground Tales

In the damp red soil at the creek's edge is a perfect set of large predator tracks made the night before. There are three crisp lobes on the bottom edge of the heel pad, denoting cat. Four toes and no claws are further indicators since cats rarely show claws unless they are running or in deep snow. These prints are roughly four inches by four inches which means cougar tracks.

The asymmetrical spread of the toes shows a middle toe and a pinky on the right end, meaning it's a right front foot. Comparing this track to other cougar tracks in my mental files, it looks like a cat that was in the 80-100 pound range, which could mean a sub-adult male or a mature female.

The last thing I examine is the relation of the front to the hind paws, which are close to each other, indicating the cat was walking. Studying the gait helps one to understand animal locomotion and determine if the critter was walking, running, loping, or stalking—essentially you are reading the stories in the tracks and, like a detective, recreating the scene in your head.

South African tracker Louis Liebenberg calls tracking humankind's first science. It is, indeed, an ancient one and our ancestors were shrewd scientists. You can see this today in watching a skilled tracker interpret the messages from the landscape—inferring, reasoning, deducing, and finally putting together a hypothesis based upon the evidence before him. There's nothing mystical about tracking though there are often amazing insights to be gleaned from the messages on the ground.

Like firemaking, tracking is a hallmark bushcraft skill. It can be used for hunting, natural history, low-impact wildlife monitoring, search and rescue, combat operations, law enforcement, or just to enhance your awareness of the creatures living under your nose.

Tracking was an ancient skill and one of humanity's first professions. It was used by hunters throughout the globe and stretches deep into human history. Nature has this habit of rooting out those who are unsuccessful and certainly hunger was and is a powerful motivator for becoming a good hunter. However, you can't be a good hunter and feed your family if you haven't first learned how to track.

Skilled trackers can decipher a wealth of signs from reading a string of animal tracks on the ground. Clues like whether the creature was male or female, old or young, running or walking, looking right or left, Democrat or Republican, and what time it passed through the region. Tracks represent only a small fragment of the story written on the ground though. Droppings, scrapes, dens, gnaw marks, chewed nuts, and antler-rubbed trees also add to the story unfolding about the hidden lives of animals.

The tracks that always make my senses bristle are those of the cougar. We have plenty of them in Arizona and they often use canyons as travel corridors. I often wonder how many times a cougar has sat atop a rocky ledge watching a group of hikers meandering below.

During a fall bushcraft course, I had to lead a student who was sick with a head cold out of our remote location. Our primitive encampment of wickiups was situated near a small river in a valley, two miles away from our vehicles. After driving the student back to town and waiting for his ride to arrive, I headed back to the desert. It was nearly 11 pm when I parked my truck amongst the clumps of creosote bushes and crucifixion thorn. A full moon had illuminated the countryside in a blue-gray hue. There was no need for a headlamp so I followed the lengthy contours of the canyon back down to our camp. Walking along the sandy bottom took some time, especially in my effort to avoid any rattlesnakes. Twice I had the sensation that something was following me.

I arrived back at camp just before 1 am and settled into my bark shelter around the fire. In the morning, my co-instructor summoned me over to a patch of ground behind our wickiups. There in the fine white sand were the distinctive tracks of a large cougar. The location of the tracks was only about twelve feet from our sleeping area. I rose and followed the prints back along the beach only to see them curve abruptly to the north.

After following the trail for a few hundred yards, I could see the cougar tracks emerging from the same canyon I had ventured down hours earlier. Upon closer inspection, I saw his tracks overlapping mine and the clear outline of where he had sat for a while observing our campsite. I can still recall the sensation of goose bumps coursing over my forearms and neck, despite the rising temperature of the desert around me. Fortunately, these big cats typically prey upon deer but it's harrowing to think that if you've spent any time hiking in the West, you've already been within striking distance of a cougar.

* * *

Cowboy Tough

Mike Landis is busy rolling a cigarette under the eaves of his rustic bunkhouse. It's something I've seen him do many times only today it is a rainy, windy, bone-chilling November as he sits unflinching just inches from the downpour coming off the rusty metal roof. His weathered skin and powerful bear-like hands are a testament to his rugged life in the wilderness. Running away from home at the age of 13, he joined a ranching outfit in Texas and never looked back.

Now at 82, he rounds up and brands cattle each year, trains horses, and tends to the rigors of daily ranch life. His wife Karen is as charismatic and knowledgeable as Mike and together they make a formidable pair of educators, showing others what traditional ranching is all about. They are cowboy-tough and my heroes and mentors in outdoor living.

Karen, by the way, is a cowboy not a cowgirl. As she says, "Cowgirls are those sparkly rodeo queens in their fancy getup, whereas cowboys like me work for a living." They have an understanding of the land that few possess and it comes from a lifetime spent amongst their surroundings. Given the physical work, grueling weather, and solitary nature, cowboying has to be the world's hardest occupation.

Ranchers in recent years have gotten a bad rap from environmentalists but you can't spend generations living on your land as a cowboy without being a good steward. You simply won't survive in the business let alone on your land. If more environmentalists spent time with people like Mike and Karen, they would understand that ranching is about more than raising cattle.

The average cowboy today makes only $750 a month which includes meals and a rustic roof over your head. There's no life or medical insurance but the state requires the rancher to pay worker's comp. In Arizona, it takes 640 acres to feed 8 cows so ranchers let their cattle roam free much of the year. When you come up on a herd, treat them with respect as they have a wild air about them, not like passive dairy cows back east.

One summer, I went out to their ranch to scout out a new location for my walkabouts. After traipsing around a tangle of parched canyons for the morning, I wound my way back to the main bunkhouse. I asked Mike if there was any water in the canyon a day's walk outback of their land. Quickly referencing the voluminous map in his head, he proceeded with hand gestures to lay out every water hole, spring, and stock tank stretching over miles of country on their land and beyond. He could even recount how productive each water source had been during the last few decades as well as wildlife one would most likely see at each location!

When he says, "I remember that spring flowing good in '69 and then after that it wasn't too consistent," you can count on it as reliable information. Such local knowledge comes only from direct experience. Mike didn't need a topo map or GPS (he had those in his head) to precisely pinpoint each water source for me and, to no surprise, his verbal descriptions later turned out to be a far better guide than the store-bought map in my hand.

Over many years of wandering and seeking out teachers of the old ways, I have met people who were deeply attuned to the rhythms of the place in which they lived. They were "natives" of their landscape as much as the willow and the raven. Spending time with people who have such intimate knowledge is one of life's greatest inspirations for me. It makes you want to stay put and learn the complexities of life in one's bio-region. There's little need for a vacation to an exotic land when there's so much to discover in the surrounding countryside.

In our 9-week Southwest Semester Program, my survival students have the luxury of spending two weeks working and living on Mike and Karen's small ranch near Seligman, Arizona. Each day brings something new but it's all hands-on whether it's shoeing a horse, fixing a fence, braiding leather, branding, or just hearing Mike recount his days cowboying around the West and in Australia.

And then there's Karen's cooking, which is otherworldly. Cowboys have to be a jacks-of-all-trades and are certainly expert at many skills but if there is one area they excel in it is eating well, and Karen holds those reins. After a hard day working in the elements, we would come back to the bunkhouse for a sumptuous meal of homemade chili (with their beef), golden cornbread made from scratch, and apple pie that you'd walk across miles of cactus for.

Mike's approach to showing others the wonders of Dutch-oven cooking is memorable. After an hour of preparing the campfire coals, he places the DOs in the fire pit. You can hear and smell the sizzling biscuits in one and bacon and eggs in the other. This is all happening while the rosy fingers of dawn are creeping over the edge of the canyon around their ranch. The birds are beginning to sing and everyone is silent as the land comes awake.

Mike removes a pouch of tobacco from his plaid shirt pocket. After rolling a cigarette, he squats down and lights it up. Then, while staring into the hot coals, he says, "Now this is what I call a biscuit-smoke. When the smoke is done the biscuits are done."

Sure enough, when the cigarette is spent, he stands and removes the Dutch ovens. After liberating the lid, the sight of golden-brown biscuits and finely done quiche draws everyone forward to the culinary delight. Mike makes such feats look easy but as he says, "It took me nine minutes and fifty-seven years to cook this here breakfast."

Postscript: Since penning this chapter, Mike Landis has taken his final ride. His truly authentic nature, humor, and deep integrity will never be forgotten. Happy trails and many good biscuit-smokes to you, Mike.

* * *
Bake, Chill, Repeat

It's April and time to collect cattail shoots for food, gather willow for basketry and arrow shafts, and yucca leaves for cordage. The wind will be with me today as it always is during the months of spring. There are very few days in the Southwest without a breeze or ferocious gust at your back.

The Hopi wind god is known as *Yapontsa* and they say he dwells in the side of an extinct volcano north of Flagstaff. Today I can feel his breath pouring over the landscape, permeating everything in his path. It shapes sand into dunes, topples towering monarchs amongst the Ponderosa pines, and scours the mesas clean of tumbleweed. The plants and trees of the desert have evolved to cope with this wind stress. Ponderosa pine and gambel oak, which grow exposed in the mountains, have spiraled grain so they don't snap in half like a tree that has straight grain. The same is true of stalks of yucca, agave, and that desert oddity, ocotillo. All have evolved in response to the breath of *Yapontsa*. The wind in the Southwest touches and shapes everything. In the town of Winslow (or *Windsblow* as the locals call it), there's a joke that one day the wind stopped blowing and seven people fell over. If you live in Arizona, you better have things tied down or stowed away unless you want it to end up in Utah. I once had a metal roof on a shed that was sheared off like it was aluminum foil during a day of 60 mph winds. Goggles, eye drops, and a shemagh are must-have items to reduce corneal abrasions, lubricate red eyes, and prevent dust inhalation.

You learn quickly that there's a reason the Hopi and Zuni build those fabulous, time-tested adobe pueblos. In the desert, the wind will test such a home's blueprint as surely as it did the ancient peoples. Another enduring design proven out under the harsh scrutiny of the natural world are shelters called wickiups which were used by native peoples as their nomadic lifestyle took them across the landscape. It is a half-tipi design made of juniper poles, brush, bark, and debris. I have slept many nights in such shelters and they shed the wind well compared to a standard lean-to.

In my classes, a group can make a wickiup large enough to comfortably sleep six people in under two hours. The wickiup was used throughout western North America and could be constructed for just one person to scrunch into or made twelve feet high with a central fire pit. Anything to prevent the far-reaching hands of Yapontsa from wringing your flesh all night.

I have seen the wind uproot mature pine trees before my eyes and send them, like ghosts, floating across the landscape to rest a quarter of a mile from whence they were born. The wind never sleeps in this land. Dust storms can cover miles in the open desert and swallow cars. Each spring, there are eighteen-wheelers blown off the interstate east of Flagstaff during ferocious windstorms.

During a spring course with a European military unit, we put together a culmination exercise on the last day that involved a series of land navigation challenges coupled with survival skills. The entire activity was to take place over eight miles and be not more than six hours in length.

The unit was split into two groups. I shadowed one group while my co-instructor Billy accompanied the other. We began around 8 am under clear skies and an already scorching sun, with temps hovering around 78 degrees. This was in a landscape of sand dunes, slick rock mesas, and snaky canyons. The sky was a classic Southwestern powder blue but many miles away to the south was a columnar storm cloud funneling up, an unusual sight for the early morning and the month of May.

I had provided each person with the same rendezvous grids for their GPS units and, after swigging down some water, we all split into our groups and set off at a trot from the vehicles. Each man was carrying their packs and supplemental gear. The emphasis, during the trek out, was on simulating an evasion scenario where they had to move quickly and minimize their visual signatures on the ground.

The desert warmed up quickly, as it always does, given the lack of immediate cloud cover and the nearby bedrock greedily absorbing the radiant heat. A few hours later, each group made it without incident to the rendezvous point, a cluster of low boulders amidst a sea of sand. They then made their evasion shelters, took some photos, and tanked up on their remaining water. Afterward, we all took a break under an overhanging ledge of Moenkopi sandstone.

While we were packing up, several dust devils swept through our shade shelter and we could see the massive storm cell in the distance changing direction and heading our way. Not wanting to get caught in the open when lightning came nor wanting to contend with the hazards of potential quicksand in the storm's aftermath, we hastily packed up.

The return route was only four miles and we headed back single file in one group. Within ten minutes, the winds had picked up significantly and created a sand storm obscuring the way. Before we were completely overtaken, we gathered in a circle and pulled out compasses, sighting in on a distant mass of immense boulders two miles away.

We agreed that we would all meet there and stick together in two-man teams while enroute. There were several geographic handrails to keep everyone from getting too lost, such as the dry riverbed to the west and a large mesa to the east. The whipping sand made breathing difficult given all the pollen, debris, insects, and dust slamming into our faces. Everyone donned shemaghs over their nose and mouth and we soon resembled a bunch of swarthy cowboys.

Visibility was reduced to a few feet and, other than constant checks on the compass bearing, the person's boots in front of me became the focal point.

Eventually the two lead soldiers pushed on to the boulders as the guys in the rear kept stopping to marvel at the storm and take pictures whenever a momentary calm presented itself. At one point, a few of us stopped by the side of a massive slab of sandstone, its form jutting upright like a spaceship that had crashed. At the base were some of the largest quartz crystals I'd ever seen, resembling milky-white carrots in the sand. This geologic treasure trove made us forget the sand scouring our faces for a few minutes before we resumed our numeric heading.

We all finally arrived at the boulder field which encompassed around a hundred acres and contained rock formations as large as a two-story building. As the sand subsided, lighting and rain swept in, pounding the region and turning the substrate into a soupy mess. The temperature had plummeted to the 50s and we had gone from combatting heat exhaustion issues to coping with the potential for hypothermia.

While cloaking ourselves in extra layers, one of the guys noticed an array of prehistoric petroglyphs on the rock panel above us. It was both an astounding and eerie sight to be engulfed in a storm and glance up to see animalistic figures peering down upon us. With little else to do until the storm subsided, we poked around the boulder field and discovered hundreds upon hundreds of rock art figures pecked into the sandstone surface. Some were serpentine while others were of hunters pursuing bighorn sheep. These were made by the ancestral Hopi who had once lived in the region.

A few hours later, the storm cell had passed and the sun emerged, heating the landscape into a searing oven over the next hour. We packed up and hiked back to the vehicles, leaving our rock art sanctuary behind. By the time we arrived at the trucks, the temperature was hovering around 101 degrees and we were gulping down water and electrolytes once more. The most humorous part of the day was when the guys thanked us for providing such a memorable experience—*like we orchestrated the sand storm!*

The wind is a part of the fabric of the Southwest as much as the rocks, canyons, and cacti. Sometimes the wind subsides and it is so still that you can have a candle lit without a flutter in its flame. You may even hear your heart beating. Such times you must remember—*Yapontsa* is just resting until tomorrow. He will return.

* * *
Gift Of The Deer

Few skills in bushcraft can equal the pleasure of fashioning your own clothes from buckskin that you tanned by hand in the old way. Braintan buckskin is a magical material and the creation of it—from rawhide to velvety soft leather—is an incredible process to behold.

Throughout North America, the fall hunt provides thousands of deer, elk, and moose hides that are often bound for the landfill. In northern Arizona, the dumpsters at the game processing shops are overflowing in November as few hunters utilize the entire animal and even fewer people tan hides traditionally, even amongst native peoples.

I have several processing shops that set aside hides for me and my students during our 9-week semester program. We can also get fresh ribcages that are discarded and we relish these for the barbecue. At one time, the entire animal was utilized for practical, ethical, and spiritual reasons. Nowadays, it's often the choice cuts of meat and the trophy head that are saved.

Ancient hunters would have procured deer with atlatls, bow and arrow, snares, pit traps, orchestrated animal drives into enclosed canyons, and even run down the animals in a lengthy endurance test. A poor shot resulted in the hunter having to track the wounded animal great distances so tremendous care in both stalking and shooting were required. There are many accounts from Supai natives in the Grand Canyon that I've spoken with where hunters, using primitive bows and arrows, made the majority of their kill shots at deer within 20 feet of the animal.

Once dispatched, the deer was then sliced open with stone tools and the entrails were removed. The deer was a hardware and grocery store for aboriginal hunters and every part of the animal had a use.

Some of the ways in which deer can be utilized:

Meat—unused portions were turned into jerky by hanging on drying racks in the sun. Typically eight hours in the desert sun would do the job. In more humid regions, the meat would have to be smoked over several days. We have made jerky in Arizona in five hours on a windy day.

Antler—could be fashioned into war clubs, spear points, and knife handles. Antlers of various sizes were also prized tools for flintknapping arrowheads.

Bones—used for fashioning arrowheads and knives, needles, awls, fishing hooks, pipes, fleshing tools, and jewelry. Ribs were turned into scrapers for tanning hides while scapulas were used for digging implements and garden hoes.

Hooves—once removed these were pounded and then boiled in water to make hide glue. Dewclaws could be strung in bundles of 20 and made into ankle rattles for dances.

Tendons—also called sinew, were pounded up to form threads for sewing, weaving bowstrings, suturing wounds, lashing arrowheads, and making into snares. This is truly the strongest natural fiber on the planet.

Stomach—deer, buffalo, elk, moose, and cows have multiple stomachs. When cleaned out and dried, they can be used for storage pouches, cooking vessels, and water containers. In Arctic regions, the intestines were sewn into waterproof anoraks for kayakers.

Brains—which have natural oils, were used for tanning the deer hide and turning it into soft, pliable leather—hence the term braintan buckskin. These were also cooked up like scrambled eggs (but with a much different taste!).

Jawbone—used as a blade for cutting plant fibers, the same thing the deer used it for. I've heard of Great Lakes tribes using beaver teeth for wood gouges and carving.

Hide—could be used for rawhide, rattles, drums, braided cord, snowshoe lacings, and moccasin soles. The braintanned hide was made into shirts, leggings, dresses, moccasins, quivers, blankets, bags, hats, loincloths, and pants.

When it comes to tanning a hide special skills and lots of elbow grease are required. When you first get the hide, it is covered with fat, meat, blood, and often ticks. After soaking the hide overnight in a creek or barrel of water to tenderize it and kill the ticks, it goes over a fleshing beam of wood and the slow, laborious process of scraping begins. As you stand over the visceral hunk of uncooperative flesh, while every fly in the state swarms around the work area, you question your intestinal fortitude and your nose's ability to regulate odor. After a three-hour (or longer for bigger hides) arm and back workout scraping off the epidermis, the hide's inner fibers are exposed and are ready for the next step of tanning with the brains.

My friend Steve Hirst, who lived with the Supai Indians in the remote western Grand Canyon in the 1960s, observed traditional brain tanning when it was still actively used in the village. He said the Supai utilized a horse rib for scraping the hair and epidermis off and then they would apply a mixture of fresh deer brains and spinal fluid. This oily mixture penetrates deep into the fibers of the hide and, after a day of stretching and softening by hand, results in beautiful leather. It's been said that every animal has enough brains to tan its own hide but ancient peoples also used bark tannins, yucca soap, and oily nuts like jojoba to produce the softening effect. The pioneers even used eggs!

If you just remove the hide from a deer, scrape off the hair and let it dry, you'll end up with rawhide (think dog bones). This material was used for drums, rattles, snowshoe bindings, cord, containers, and the soles of moccasins. But no one wants to wear a rawhide loincloth so adding the brains is essential for producing soft leather.

After brain tanning, the finished hide needed to be smoked to preserve the brains within the fiber structure and ensure that the garment dried soft should it get wet. Smoking took about thirty minutes over the coals which were covered with rotten chunks of wood. Some tribes like the Hopi and Supai desired pure white buckskin for ceremonial garments so the hide was left unsmoked and rubbed with white clay.

Whether made from deer, antelope, elk, cougar, or even squirrel, tanned hides provided warm and durable clothing like no other material found in nature. The process of making traditionally tanned leather is laborious but nothing is more amazing than to take part in transforming a raw deer hide into buttery-soft leather. From the time you remove the hide from the deer until the finished product is in your hands, you are looking at roughly two days of arm-wrenching work.

When I hold a finished piece of buckskin in my hands, I think of the miles that the deer traveled over in its lifetime out on the land, how many times its fine senses enabled it to elude coyotes and cougars, and of the movement of wind, sand, snow, and sun on its body while living under open skies from birth to death. My own body has been constructed on the flesh of this animal and I am always grateful when partaking of a meal of venison from a creature that once gazed upon the same sunsets as I do.

Today there are many people I know who wear buckskin as their only garment and haven't dressed in *regular* clothing in 20 years or more. Of course, keeping in mind that we have over 100,000 generations of ancestors who wore animal skins, the term *regular clothing* could be debated. Buckskin holds up extremely well; after all, the deer wore it on their backs for an entire lifetime.

A single deer hide that has been braintanned can fetch up to $220 while elk goes for around $40 and a luxurious buffalo hide with the hair on can sell for $1000. To completely clothe yourself in the old way using braintanned deer hides, you would need eight skins. Two skins to make a sleeveless shirt, three skins for a warm long-sleeved overshirt, two large skins for a pair of pants, and one skin for moccasins, pouches, etc... Now, imagine if you are in a hunting-gathering band of 25 people and you will see that game procurement was something you did constantly and in every season.

This tally of skins is impressive but bear in mind that it doesn't include the buffalo robes of the Great Plains, polar bear skin pants in the Arctic, or rabbit skin blankets in the high desert. A 4'x4' rabbit skin robe would require 150 such hides. I recall one Navajo man saying that his grandfather's most treasured possession, in days past, was his packrat skin blanket comprised of over 350 rat hides! It is easy to scoff at such a thing until you have spent time on the brutally cold mesas of the Four Corners region where the wind never sleeps.

When I work so hard on tanning and then tailoring a shirt, it can be shocking to stroll into town and walk through a clothing store with dozens of racks of shirts that were repetitiously stamped out in an overseas factory. How quickly life has changed for us modern humans in the course of a few thousand years or even a few generations as is the case in the Southwest, where many native peoples were living off the land full-time until recently.

As of late, brain tanning has seen a remarkable comeback as evidenced by the many full-time traditional tanners. My friends who tan for a living say their number one group of clients are Native peoples, where the skill has largely faded, and the second group is the Mountain Man re-enactors. If you are in transition between careers, there's always the arm-wrenching occupation of brain tanning to consider. On the bright side, you'll never have to pay for your clothes again.

* * *

The Amazing Cowpie Firemaking Technique

"This is Echo Charlie One, calling in for instructions, over," said the raspy voice of Frank, a Special Forces soldier on the other end. He was on day three of his five-day survival solo in the high desert. The day before, the Sgt. Major and I had made a surprise visit to everyone's primitive camps in the canyon below our basecamp. We informed them that they had *accidentally* lost all of their knives, firemaking tools, and rucksack. The rest of their solo would require them to use primitive stone tools, friction firemaking implements, and an improvised backpack since we'd be removing the other items. These were all skills we had previously covered during a four-day instructional period prior to their solo.

"Open envelope #21," replied the Sgt. Major on his radio, "and then call back once you've completed the assigned task."

We provided each participant with a Ziploc bag that contained 30 envelopes with a variety of survival tasks. Some of these were simple like carving a throwing stick or making deadfall traps. Others, like the contents of envelope #21, were more advanced. This particular task involved Frank locating suitable wood to carve a bow-drill firemaking set. Once his fire was made, he was to call back in for further instructions.

As the morning unfolded, the other five operators radioed in upon completion of their tasks. Frank however was not to be heard from. Finally, around noon, he called. In a low, sullen voice, he indicated that he could not get a fire started using bow-drill or even hand-drill, the latter method he had resorted to after much frustration and cussing with the previous approach (he recounted later). Though there was still an inkling of determination in his voice, his mood was somber.

The Sgt. Major instructed him to open envelope #28. The envelope numbers seemed random but the tasks inside were sequential and all contained on a master list at our basecamp. This helped keep participants who decided to inspect all of their envelopes on the first day from anticipating what task was coming next.

This particular envelope instructed Frank with the following: "Using the fire you've just obtained by primitive means, you must now boil water in your canteen cup. Upon completion, radio in for your next set of instructions."

After Frank had read the contents of the envelope, there was a very long pause and then he finally ground out his solemn reply, "Copy that… copy that. Echo Charlie One out."

An hour later, the radio crackled and Frank replied with great enthusiasm that his objective had been met. I could almost hear him grinning through the speaker. He was instructed to open a new envelope with a set of compass bearings for navigating to his next camp location.

The next day, we did a safety check on everyone in their individual camps and found Frank sitting in his bark shelter with a cocky smirk. I asked him if it was bow-drill or hand-drill that had enabled him to finally obtain his fire. "Neither—I used this instead," he said, reaching down and pulling a mud-encrusted pair of binoculars out of his shelter.

"I found these binos two days earlier near a spring in a side canyon. I reckon they must've been dropped by a dayhiker." He began unscrewing the right eyepiece and then knelt down beside a cowpie to demonstrate his technique. "I used it like a magnifying lens to get a cowpie smoldering and then put a bunch of bark over it to ignite the ember. Then I boiled up my water as per the instructions."

With my eyebrows raised in wonder, I said it's always better to be lucky than skilled but in his case he excelled at both. Now, when we teach a class, we always tell the story about Frank's amazing optical cowpie firemaking technique and all of the random variables involved.

* * *

Three Dog Night

It's February and the snow hasn't stopped falling in two days. When most folks think of Arizona, they conjure up images of columnar cacti amidst sweltering sand dunes and slickrock. But at an elevation of 7000' here in the mountains in Flagstaff, it sure isn't very toasty come winter time.

As I peck these words out on the keyboard, cozy in our well-insulated strawbale house in the woods, I can see our four dogs sprawled around the family room floor. They are trusted family members who have accompanied me on many survival outings. They allow my senses to extend into the natural world, taking in scent and sound that would otherwise go unnoticed. I wouldn't be the woodsman I am without them.

My dogs always sleep beside me on backcountry trips and I have long had an appreciation for the Basque sheepherders in these mountainous regions who treasured their dogs' warmth on a cold night. According to the local sheepherder's lore, if it is 32 degrees out or more, then it's a one dog night; below freezing is a two dog night; and when it gets below zero, then you better have three big dogs under your blankets! The temperature gauge outside our window indicates that tonight is going to be a three dog night for sure. Most of the dogs in northern Arizona are "rez" dogs, that is off the Indian reservation, and mine are no exception. There's no shortage of rez dogs in Arizona. The majority we see up here are Australian Shepherd, Heeler, or Border Collie mixes due to the number of both Anglo and Navajo ranches. Strangely enough, there is also a concentration of Rhodesian Ridgeback mixes.

Rez dogs are special and their loyalty is absolutely unwavering, more so than other dogs I've known. They are so appreciative to have a good home because many have endured a brutal life, fending for themselves in the wilds or on the fringe of reservation towns. Those pups that survive to adulthood have had to battle or avoid almost daily encounters with coyotes, packs of feral dogs, cougars, rattlesnakes, intense heat, biting cold, dehydration, and unfriendly two-leggeds. The overpopulation problem on reservations in the western U.S. is staggering. Most rez dogs in Arizona don't live past the age of two according to one vet I spoke with in the Four Corners region. The problems are manyfold such as lack of funds for spaying/neutering, tribal laws prohibiting stray dogs from being removed by outsiders, apathy towards dogs in some towns, and then the extreme heat and cold which take a heavy toll.

Our latest pup that we rescued recently was an Aussie Shepherd/ Rat Terrier mix—an odd combination indeed. She was emaciated and, at ten weeks old, showed the ravages and scars from having to fight off adult dogs and coyotes to stay alive. The vet informed us she had worms, giardia, mange, and other problems associated with a life of scavenging. When we brought her home, she lay around the house for probably eight weeks before her immune system recovered. Initially, I thought she was just a passive pup but after regaining her strength, she resembled a pinball, bouncing around the house much to the displeasure of my older dogs. She is one of the most amazing hunters I've encountered and can catch squirrels on the run. Like many small dogs (twenty pounds), she doesn't seem to realize her diminutive nature around others of her kind and likes them to know that she's the boss. If you are ever passing through the Southwest and are in search of a gem of a dog, stop in at one of the rescue shelters and adopt a rez dog.

One thing I will say about a pooch that was born and raised in the wilds is that they are housebroken in a day or two because they know that the outside is where they are supposed to relieve themselves. Rez dogs are also incredible hunters, having acquired the prowess of a wild predator. While I bring dog food on extended trips, my dogs won't touch it during an entire week afield. Their fare consists of lizards, rabbits, and other wild game obtained on the move.

On the Navajo reservation, near the town of Pinon, there is a cave in a remote stretch of high desert where archeologists found two dog mummies amidst human burials during an excavation in the 1930s. The place is called "White Dog Cave" and the dog remains date back to 600 AD. I have long bought into the old research which suggests that humans domesticated dogs and they evolved alongside us. In recent years, my thinking has changed as dog behaviorists and biologists now surmise that the human/canid relationship was one of co-evolution and co-domestication. That makes more sense to me given how much both species depend on each other, especially when afield.

Living in Flagstaff, you are in the minority if you have fewer than two dogs. Walk through downtown on a Saturday afternoon and you will be in dog heaven as pooches pull their humans to and fro. Why, we even have two "bark parks" that the city designed for dogs to unwind off leash. Of course, my dogs must think they're already in paradise with the daily romps through the woods, endless deer hides to chew on from my tanning work, the abundant squirrel population that borders our land, and the countless students who dote upon them during fieldcourses.

Given how much I work and travel on the reservations in the Southwest, we would have ten more dogs in the house if I had the means of fostering them. However, when this last pup arrived, and after my wife removed her hands from my throat, I promised that we would stop at four.

I grew up with a malamute that was a cherished friend to the end and I am forever grateful for the world of canids. It is an ancient connection and one that ties us even further to our wild heritage. The only problem with four dogs is that you need a revolving door as one of them always needs to go outside. Looks like it's time to don the winter garb and greet the white stuff beyond the window. The pack has already gathered.

* * *

When Yucca Was King

Yucca, Spanish bayonet, datil, soapweed—all names for one of the most important plant resources used by ancient peoples in the Southwest. There was a time when yucca was king and it literally wove together the day-to-day life of the prehistoric cultures. If you were an ancient traveler in the desert regions a thousand years ago, yucca would have been a critical plant ally providing the means to fashion rope, tumplines, baskets, sandals, fire by friction, soap, medicine, and offering carbohydrate-rich fruits. It was and still is a tremendously utilized plant in the Southwest though its applications today, amongst native peoples, are now most often associated with basketry.

A member of the Lily family, the genus Yucca includes about 40 species, most of which are found in the Southwest and Mexico, although some species are indigenous to the southeastern United States and the Caribbean islands. Yucca grows on windswept mesas, in the low desert, and can even be found up to 8500 feet on the San Francisco Peaks of northern Arizona.

One use for this amazing plant is in the area of primitive firemaking—otherwise known as the *art of rubbing two sticks together.* Archeological evidence indicates that the predominant method of firemaking used throughout the Southwest, before the Bic, was the friction method called the hand-drill.

I remember the first time I used yucca for firemaking in the old way. It was on a 10-day primitive walkabout in central Arizona where a friend and I were relying solely on the ancient skills used in the Southwest without the aid of any modern gear. With sunset upon us and a cold night ahead, we were on a quest for fire and sought out a cluster of narrow leaf yuccas with dead stalks.

After cutting down a weathered stalk with my blade, I sharpened the pithy stalk into a flat fireboard and carved out a small hole with a notch. This hole would receive a spindle made from another thin yucca stalk. Thirty seconds of twirling the spindle into the fireboard and a glowing coal was produced which was then placed in a bundle of shredded cottonwood bark and blown into flame. We were no longer at the mercy of the cold and a dinner of cactus fruit, mesquite flour, and panfish cooked over the open flames never tasted so good.

Fire by friction is one skill that was certainly used by prehistoric peoples and making it with your own hands is an empowering feeling that connects you with an ancient timeline. Ever since that trip, I have always looked upon yucca with great appreciation and respect.

The hand-drill method universally employs three underlying principles that are critical to success:

1) Soft, non-resinous wood like yucca or cottonwood must be used.

2) A skillful combination of speed and downward pressure must be employed if the proper level of friction is to occur.

3) And lots of elbow grease coupled with hand callouses are involved.

A couple of things become evident when you first undertake primitive firemaking. The first is that you can give up your gym membership. The second is that you will never be caught in the wilds without a lighter! You wouldn't want to perform this method if you were truly in a survival situation. Finally, a lot of "P's" go into primitive firemaking—perspiration, persistence, patience, practice, and, in the event of rain, *prayer*. Friction firemaking certainly does give you a healthy respect for the day-to-day living skills used by our ancestors.

If you want to try this method of firemaking, you will need three materials: a hand-drill, a fireboard, and a tinder bundle.

First, cut a plant stalk for the drill. This needs to be about 16" long and made from yucca, sunflower, mullein, seep willow, arrow wood, or cattail. The most common material showing up in the ethnographic literature in Arizona is yucca. Back in Michigan I used mullein and cattail stalks.

Second, carve a flat fireboard of soft, non-resinous wood such as yucca, cottonwood, aspen, or willow. Avoid resinous wood such as pine as the sap will cause convective cooling and not allow for the formation of a coal. Specimens from the Museum of Northern Arizona were made from yucca and juniper. My personal favorite is to use cottonwood for a fireboard with a drill made from a seep-willow stalk.

Third, construct a tinder bundle from the fluffy shredded bark of a dead juniper or cottonwood tree. Form it into a bird's nest and use it to cradle the coal before sending it on its way to flame.

Finally, practice, practice, practice—this is a skill that the ancient peoples of the Southwest used on a daily basis so it takes time to develop proficiency. Oh yeah, lots of caveman grunting help too.

Another use for yucca is to make soap. It doesn't take much to create some quick suds for your hair or hands. The entire plant contains saponins and is one of the few wild plants that can be used as a soap substitute. When out on a long primitive trek with a group, my students often strongly encourage each other to gather some yucca root after day four!

The waxy green coating on yucca leaves can be utilized for a quickie lather. When I make rope from the inner fibers of yucca, I always save this green fuzz. This is easily shaved off with a stone flake or a knife held at a right angle. The most concentrated soap, however, can be had from the yucca root. Rather than dig up or injure an entire plant just for a small root section, I prefer to look for yuccas overhanging rock faces or outcroppings where the roots are already exposed. I then carefully cut a small thumb-sized piece as this will not damage the plant. Better yet, look for yuccas that have been uprooted by skunks or javelinas. Even roots from dead yuccas can be used. Next, the root is sliced up and then mashed in about two cups of water. Voila—wilderness shampoo. Who said you can't smell good in the outback!

Using yucca to make fire in the old way or to weave with are ways of gaining a deeper connection to the desert landscape as well as providing insight into prehistoric living that you can't get walking through a museum. Every environment found in North American had a key plant or animal resource that stood out above the others and became the crucial link for the ancient cultures to thrive in that region. For the Plains Indians it was the buffalo, for the Inuit of the interior Arctic it was the caribou, for Northwest Coast tribes it was the cedar tree and salmon. In the Southwest, it was yucca. Yucca was king.

* * *

Al Sieber: Master of Bushcraft

Everyone who ventures into the world of bushcraft has a hero who sums up what it means to walk the walk. An aspiring bushcrafter should delve into the figures of Jim Corbett, Dick Proenneke, Calvin Rutstrum, Nessmuk, Adrian Boshier, Dan Beard, Horace Kephardt, Victorio, Kent Frost, Warren Miller, and others.

However, one unsung hero is the tough-as-nails tracker, Al Sieber, who is my personal favorite. From 1871 to 1886, he was the chief of Apaches Scouts under General George Crook and a pivotal figure in the unfolding of the Apache Campaign in Arizona.

Traveling through the parched Southwest, with its miles of cacti, rock escarpments, and scarcity of water makes you realize how harsh the land must have been for the thousands of U.S. troops stationed here during the Apache Wars. During the Geronimo Campaign of the 1880s, a typical soldier had post-civil war garments consisting of wool fatigues, black boots, rifle, rations, and seventy pounds of gear for the field. The most amazing thing was the fact that each man was only issued a single metal one-quart canteen! Commanding officers discovered that during some of the more brutal summer campaigns there would be a twenty percent attrition rate from heat stroke when garrisons were sent out to the field. Officers at Fort Verde, where many of the campaigns against the Apaches were launched, knew that two men out of ten would not return from routine patrols due to death from heat stroke or dehydration.

General Crook, the commanding officer at Fort Verde, referred to the Apaches as the "tigers of the human race," such was his respect for them. He knew that to catch an Apache you had to use an Apache. Towards this end, he enlisted other Apaches from rival bands and used their tracking skills and knowledge of the desert to hunt down Geronimo and his band of followers. The person responsible for leading these Apache scouts in pursuit of Geronimo was Al Sieber. His official title was civilian chief of scouts for the U.S. Army. While Geronimo permeates the historical literature of the Southwest, Sieber was the legendary tracker whose leadership and bushcraft skills earned him the respect of his Apache scouts and is partly connected with the surrender of Geronimo.

As his biographer Daniel Thrapp points out, "His position was the

most eminently hazardous post held by any white man in the Southwest."
In my mind, he was perhaps the most pivotal figure in the ending of the
Apache Wars and the opening (or closing depending on your point of
view) of the Southwest. He was certainly one of Arizona's most amazing
frontiersmen and a part of the larger American westward expansion.

Sieber was a tough hombre for sure. In his two decades of fighting in
the Apache Wars and many close scrapes with death, he had over twen-
ty-nine knife, arrow, and bullet scars tattooing his leathery exterior. Whenever he was injured in the field, he would often apply a hot rod to cauterize
the wound and then head back out in pursuit of his prey.

Actor Robert Duvall masterfully played him in the movie *Geronimo,*
An American Legend. With the exception of one directorial mistruth where
Sieber dies in a bar in Mexico after a shootout, the script is almost entirely
based upon the non-fiction book, *The Truth About Geronimo*, written by Lt.
Britton Davis who fought alongside Sieber.

What amazes me is how few people, outside of the Apaches, know
about him, even lifelong Arizonans. One summer, I was visiting a friend
who lives in a tipi in the Superstition Mountains near Roosevelt Lake which
is around 100 miles east of Phoenix. On my return trip home, I had hoped
to find the monument to Sieber, which was supposed to have been located
off the shores of the lake. I had sought out many of the battlefields that
Sieber had been at but had not been able to locate that last place where he
stood before meeting his bizarre ending. A roadside monument in such
a remote area seems like a strange place to look for the marker of a man
who was so instrumental in Arizona history. However, fate was not kind to
Sieber in his final days.

With the burgeoning metropolis of Phoenix in need of another reliable water source, the Roosevelt dam was proposed to contain the flow
of the Salt River. During the early 20th century, it was to be the largest
concrete dam in the world. Laborers were needed to pave the road for its
construction and Sieber was responsible for overseeing a workforce of
Apaches, some of whom he had formerly commanded decades earlier.

On a winter day in February, he rose to greet the dawn in what would
be his last salutation.

He rode down from his cabin on his horse to the scene below where
the workers had gathered. After dismounting, he stood on the narrow dirt
road. A few minutes later, while overlooking the windswept valley below,
a loose boulder fell from above and crushed him. Some accounts say that
it was a bizarre mishap and others say that a few Apaches, bitter towards

Sieber for his past involvement in the Apache Campaign, dislodged the boulder. Either way, that was the end of the legendary chief of scouts. He is buried in Globe, Arizona, south of where he met his demise.

While driving back home, I stopped at a Forest Service building near the Roosevelt dam, to inquire about that spot where the boulder plummeted down. I approached several officials who manage the federal lands only to have them scratch their heads when I asked if they knew of the marker commemorating the famous chief of scouts. I stopped at a local RV campground to ask the owner if he knew of the location but met with the same reaction. Discouraged, I drove north on Highway 188 back to Flagstaff. After passing over the dam bridge, I suddenly spied a rock monument of some sort on a gravel overlook above the banks of the lake.

Sure enough, the four-foot-high marker was dedicated to Sieber. Meandering over to the solitary pillar, I could see a bronze plaque with an inscription that read: "Al Sieber, veteran of the Civil War and for twenty years a leader of scouts for the U.S. Army in Arizona Indian troubles, was killed on this spot February 19, 1907 by a rolling rock during construction of the Tonto Road."

What an ending for such a bushman. Life is strange and it has always struck me that Sieber, who was a soldier, logger, mountain man, trapper, and Apache fighter was a victim of geologic and gravitational forces at this very spot.

I took off my hat and silently nodded to the old warrior. Somewhere above I could hear the shrill of a red-tailed hawk that was floating above the whole scene. Looking back at the monument, I was surprised at the pleasing sight to the rear of the marker. Resting atop the rock column was a bouquet of fresh flowers. I smirked and figured that at least one other person in Arizona must know about him.

This isn't the only indicator left as a reminder of the man who helped shape so much of our Southwestern history. There is also Sieber Creek near the East Fork of the Verde River and Sieber Point on the north rim of the Grand Canyon. If you want some fascinating reading about a tumultuous period in the American Southwest, check out Dan Thrapp's fine historical work, *Al Sieber, Chief of Scouts*. It will thrust you into the heart of cactus country and provide you with insight into the life of this master of bushcraft.

* * *

The Schism Between Worlds

Red streaks of light snake across the morning sky and illuminate the sprawling walls of the sandstone canyon. I'm hiking through a cathedral of cottonwood trees which line the canyon floor after finishing a seven-day primitive walkabout. Armed with little more than the dusty clothes on my back and a small daypack of critical items, I am, as my good friend and longtime guide Randy Miller would say, preparing for "re-entry" into the civilized world. I think often of those words on such treks. I'm afraid that it's true that many of us who guide for a living have difficulty parting at season's end with our favorite wilderness sanctuary, be it a mountain range, canyon, desert, or forest.

In the sandy contours of this canyon, tracks reveal themselves: the paw prints of a bobcat, gray fox, skunk, numerous lizards, and the ubiquitous raccoon. I pause to interpret the manuscript on the ground before me. Mostly I just want to soak up the morning sun on my face and shake off the chill from last night. The past seven days have been an up and down of balmy weather and torrential rains, typical of this land of extremes. Coyotes and ravens will accompany you day and night in this land so you are never truly alone. A day in the elements is a day to long for and I'll take as many as life blesses me with.

Strangely, the day after this trek ends, I will be driving through the inner bowels of Los Angeles to attend a friend's wedding. Being an outdoor educator, particularly a survival instructor where you are taking care of life's basic priorities from sunup to sundown means that you are sometimes embracing a schizophrenic lifestyle as you try to transition from the wilderness to the "other" world of human design. This distinction between the two worlds of nature and civilization becomes dramatically apparent to those of us who guide for a living.

I remember a bushcraft course I taught one summer where six of us were living primitively for a week in the wilds while relying on our survival skills and what the land offered. Each day we were sleeping in handmade shelters, making fire in the old way, navigating with the sun and stars, gathering edible plants, fashioning bows and arrows, and just living in the moment.

After seven days of glorious weather, communal work, and much fine dining on wild foods, the course ended. We drove back to Flagstaff, said our goodbyes, and then our small tribe departed with hugs. Two hours later at home, I was changing diapers, answering phone calls, and sifting through email. As one old river guide here said, "This occupation—living constantly out of your pack between two worlds—causes you to be schizophrenic for much of the year."

Having seen what happens to full-time guides and river runners whose occupation becomes all consuming, I realized that there was a decision to be made between choosing to work on perfecting my craft or choosing to work on perfecting my life. A few years after becoming a parent, the decision to reduce my teaching load became much easier for me. Though I had to run a certain number of courses in order to make a living at what I love doing, I didn't want to be the guide who missed his child's birthdays and precious years because I was worried about getting in just "one more adventure."

After sifting through the array of paw prints painted on the ground before me, I continue north towards a small spring. Alongside the path are Christmas tree chollas, hedgehog cacti, and the occasional mesquite tree. The Southwest is a land where everything pokes, pierces, stabs, or impales. Mindfulness is required for hiking in these parts and it's not hard to understand why many desert tribes here had taboos about wandering around at night.

Looking up the canyon, I spot a lush hackberry tree with its serpentine arms draped over a rocky outcropping. Such an immense tree residing in a parched landscape required investigation and I clambered up the rocky slope. Under the shade of the tree's canopy was a large pool of fresh water that emanated from a spring below the roots. A look in every direction revealed only boulders and sand but here, in this place, was a source of life and comfort. My slightly parched throat reminds me that it's time to fill up on water and to give silent thanks for this precious substance that ushers forth from the earth and brings beauty to the land. With the sun on my face, water on my lips, and birdsong in the air, I am a rich man.

With my guiding season nearly over, I think of the winter months ahead and look forward to hibernating from teaching, at least for a while. Teaching is my calling in life and I plan on doing it until my bones feed the ground, but at the end of a long season of looking out for others, I long for the silence of winter and the pleasure of walking alone on the land.

Sometimes when the rain is howling down on my bark shelter all night long while the campfire sputters to stay aflame or I'm trying to emit a smile at having to eat another bowl of acorn mush, I question my career choice. Then a student delights in getting their first bow-drill fire or in fashioning a willow basket; or after a grueling land navigation trek, the group arrives at a freshwater spring below a tawny mesa while the rosy fingers of dusk wash over the boulders around us. Those are the things that make this more than just an outdoor job.

The sun is needling its way into my skin and the birds and lizards are already getting shade hungry. Time to head up and out of the canyon—time to head home—time for re-entry.

An ephemeral water source from a recent flash flood.

Bow-drill fire using a yucca drill on a yucca fireboard.

Slickrock country where I spend a lot of time on solos.

A Hopi-style bread oven we made at our basecamp.

Land navigation refresher with a military unit.

San Juan River country.

Kai — my trusted companion. I found him nearly dead from dehydration
in the desert after someone abandoned him.

Working with your hands is always a pleasure.

Two affectionate horses at the Landis ranch who
thought I was a treat-dispenser.

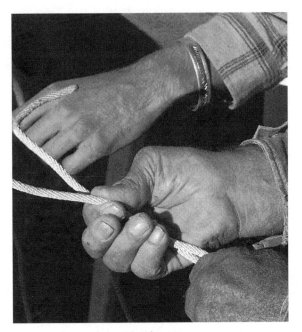

Cowboys!

Banana yucca leaves woven into cordage.

A Paiute deadfall trap used by desert cultures for
procuring small game.

The Southwest is an archeological wonderland.

Precious tinajas, or water pockets, in the sandstone.

Fun with 550 cord.

Scraping the raw deerhide to remove the epidermis before braintanning.

The finished products. Each hide is the result of two days
of arm-wrenching work.

AL SIEBER *

VETERAN OF THE
CIVIL WAR AND FOR
TWENTY YEARS A
LEADER OF SCOUTS
FOR THE U.S. ARMY
IN ARIZONA INDIAN
TROUBLES, WAS
KILLED ON THIS SPOT
FEBRUARY 19TH 1907
BY A ROLLING ROCK
DURING CONSTRUCT-
ION OF THE TONTO
ROAD

HIS BODY IS BURIED
IN THE CEMETERY AT
GLOBE

Lean-tos have kept me warm on many nights below freezing
without a sleeping bag.

A desert hairy-scorpion I found under my bedroll in the morning.

Cowboy ingenuity–a slot canyon partially filled with a few cars
and then compacted with dirt.

A Navajo sweat lodge.

About the Author

Tony Nester is the author of numerous books and DVDs on survival. His school *Ancient Pathways* is the primary provider of survival training for the Military Special Operations community and he has served as a consultant for the NTSB, FAA, Travel Channel, NY Times, Backpacker Magazine, and the film *Into the Wild*. For years he wrote a popular monthly column for Outside Magazine and his freelance writing is frequently featured in numerous print publications.

Additional Survival Books by Tony Nester:

Survival Gear You Can Live With

A Vehicle Survival Kit You Can Live With

When the Grid Goes Down: Disaster Gear and Survival Preparations for Making Your Home Self-Reliant

Bushcraft Tips & Tools

The Modern Hunter-Gatherer: A Practical Guide to Living Off the Land

Desert Survival Tips, Tricks, & Skills